YOU:

THE STING OPERATIVE

100 TACTICS TO CHANGE THE WORLD
RIGHT FROM YOUR OWN NEIGHBORHIVE

AMANDA M. FERRIS

BEAVER'S POND
PRESS

Cover Design by ChristaReedPhotography.com

ISBN 13: 978-1-59298-628-6
Library of Congress Catalog Number: 2016920156
Printed in the United States of America
First Printing: 2017
21 20 19 18 17   5 4 3 2 1

Book Design by Tiffany Daniels
Edited by Wendy Weckwerth

Beaver's Pond Press, Inc.
7108 Ohms Lane
Edina, MN 55439-2129
(952) 829-8818

www.BeaversPondPress.com
To order, visit www.ItascaBooks.com or call (800) 901-3480.

# DEDICATION

This tactical guide is dedicated to all the brave men and women (and their families) who serve our country and communities locally and abroad.

I want to express my deepest gratitude for your sacrifice, dedication, courage, and service. We can all change the world right from our own neighborhives, but we wouldn't be able to do so if it weren't for all you give and have given.

In recognition of a few heroes from my hive:

Captain George Ferris, Medical Corps, US Army 577th Motor Ambulance Company, AMEDD Silver Star, World War II

Sergeant Robert Ferris, Bloomington, MN, Police Department, Retired

E-7 Sergeant First Class Thomas Ferris, US Army National Guard Reserves, Retired

SPC/5 Robert Young, US Army First Infantry Division

Staff Sergeant Jeff Ferris, US Army 101st Airborne, Retired

Sergeant Garry Moore, Deptford, NJ, Police Department, Retired

JR Moore, US Army

Jason Rumaker, US Marine Corps

Kyle Young, US Navy

Andrew Young, US Navy

Thank you all, and may God bless you abundantly.

ACKNOWLEDGMENTS

Thank you to each person in my family—especially my mother, Susan Ferris-Moore, for your constant love and support at my rock bottom. Thank you, Mom and Dad, for your steady example of generosity and kindness to others throughout your lives. I'm so grateful for all you've taught me.

Thank you to the early leaders and mentors in my life, including David W. Anderson and family, Dave Von Rueden, Scott Schlachter, Chris Katayama, and Don Peters. Thank you to the Lifeskills Center for Leadership trainers Lisa Ripken, James Anderson, and Terri Uy-Lennon.

Special thanks to Brandon W. Johnson for your encouragement, wisdom, teaching, and truth-filled energy along the way. I'm so very fortunate to have you as a mentor and friend. To the Heart of a Leader Graduates, Warriors, and Positive-Energy People—thank you for your continued inspiration and heart. You're truly a powerful force in the positive-energy revolution!

Long-distance gratitude to Grandpa Nelson for being my biggest fan and for helping me learn the power of generosity and belief—when they're combined, we can accomplish absolutely anything we set our minds to. Thank you for cheering me (and so many other young student athletes) on during your time on this earth. I look forward to sharing "hive fives" in the sky someday. You're a legendary superhero among heroes.

Thank you to Sean Murphy for showing understanding and sharing wisdom during my dark times; your kindness encouraged me to start believing in myself and hope again. And thanks to the whole Famous Dave's family—with a special shout-out to Ted Coulter, Mike Wright, John Glockner, Randy Jernberg, and the good people of DTSG and River Valley BBQ—you're phenomenal human beings, and I'm so grateful for each and every one of you! Grace and Dustin Vanase of Bare Honey, and the great leaders and students of BestPrep—thank you for your blazing light, and thank you for the honor of passing the torch to the next generation.

To Paul Blanchard and Dave Blanchard from the Og Mandino Leadership Institute—thank you for the Intentional Creation Assessment, but more importantly, for your authenticity and support at just the right time. Huge thanks to Loffler Companies for your commitment to making a difference in the community—as an organization and as individuals. Thank you to the wonderful Wendy Fraser and Bryony Stark, as well as the entire family of Northern Lights Ballroom. I appreciate the encouragement and opportunities you provided as I was working on the Beeing Blessed Project.

Michelle Prince, Stacy Colgin, and the amazing people of Prince Performance Group—you're all so gifted and inspirational. Thank you for being a brilliant light in the world as you develop the game changers of our time! Thank you to one of my biggest heroes, Zig Ziglar, for your life of service, and the powerful legacy the Ziglar organization continues to carry beyond your time here.

To Hanna Kjeldbjerg, Wendy Weckwerth, Tiffany Daniels, Athena Currier, and the wonderful team at Beaver's Pond Press; and Keegan Johnson, Luke Warkenthien, and Christa Reed for all your behind-the-scenes ninja work. You guys rock, and I'm so lucky to have use of your superpowers on the Beeing Blessed Project. Thank you!

With my deepest gratitude, I wish to acknowledge the following individuals I'm honored to call friends. Without you all, I wouldn't be here today: Sarah

Jones-Larson and Dave Larson, Charity Wefel and Nate Wefel, Savannah Lee Jamieson and Aaron Luis Rodriguez, Jessica Falk, Amy Hayes, Jennifer Holtz, Kathy Taylor, Rachel Murphy, and to the unnamed folks who've cheered me on without judgment during my darkest hours—thank you for believing in me.

Thank You to our Creator for this beautiful life, opportunities to serve using the gifts You've entrusted us with, and each breath You give us! Thank You for the miracles in my life and using my life as a vessel to share Your love. All is possible, but only by the grace of God!

PRAISE FROM "FAMOUS" DAVE

A number of years ago I met a very enthusiastic young lady who brightened up every room she walked into. Like all of us, she went through some very difficult challenges and adversities in her life. But I was encouraged to discover that Amanda Ferris, much like myself, had used her adversities to come to a deeper, more meaningful understanding of her own true self. In this amazing transformation Amanda had an enlightening real-ization of how the honey bee—which should not fly by all scientific laws of physics—not only flies, but, through pollination, has a deeper relationship to how we all live.

Amanda's book, *YOU: The Sting Operative*, was not only a very encouraging and inspiring read, it hit the most important breakthrough truth that I had come to understand in my own life: if you want to change things in your own life, become obsessively devoted to bettering the lives of others!

We live in changing and challenging times, and having served the White House with a Presidential Appointment by President George W. Bush as Assistant Sec-retary in the United States Department of Interior, I came back from Washington D.C. understanding one unfortunate thing: our government in Washington D.C., while the greatest in the world, is gridlocked. The real strength of America has always been that each one of us can directly impact what happens in our own community, or as Amanda so aptly describes, our "own hive." We all matter, and you can make a difference in more ways than you ever imagined.

If you're looking to jumpstart your life or your career, take the lessons of the honey bee and "bee" the buzz in your own neighborhood. Get this book now and devour it—I recommend it highly!

> *Rib-O-Liciously Yours,*
> "Famous Dave" Anderson, America's Rib King
> Founder and Chairman Emeritus, Famous Dave's of America, Inc.

# FOREWORD

It was a memorable day when I was blessed to meet Mandy Ferris at one of Michelle Prince's Book Bound Workshops. As published authors, we were both featured in *Dare to Be a Difference Maker Volume 5*. Mandy's winsome smile and bigger-than-life personality are only surpassed by her compassionate heart. Mandy's passion is to change the world one person at a time, and her lifetime of experience in service to others makes her an authority on the subject.

As a side note, I found it interesting to learn on Wikipedia that the *Ferris Wheel* or *Big Wheel* rides are found at *Amusement Parks*—Mandy is certainly a *big wheel* and she is most *amusing*!

Mandy's book, *YOU: The Sting Operative—100 Tactics to Change the World,* not only gives direction on how to serve effectively, but even provides templates for organizing work to achieve greater success.

As a retired police sergeant, Mandy grabbed my attention when she told me she wanted to help our military veterans, law enforcement officers, firefighters, and their respective families. Our military and law enforcement officers live lives of service and sacrifice for our communities and our country. I am proud to support Mandy's efforts to reach out to our warrior community, and I thank God for her heart to serve these warriors.

This book contains 100 different ways that we can show love in our communities with acts of kindness towards our neighbors. The projects in the following pages can be used by individuals, as well as by organizations that do group community service projects, like Sunday schools, churches, and Girl Scouts or Boy Scouts. These acts of kindness can also extend to the workplace and beyond.

My hope is that you will find even more ways to serve others in your community, and encourage them to pay it forward—which in turn, helps make the world a better place, starting in your own backyard.

Richard M. Morris

Texas deputy constable, police chaplain, and Ziglar Legacy Certified coach

ABOUT RICHARD MORRIS

After retiring as the Gang Intelligence and Detective Sergeant following nearly thirty-six years with the Fort Worth Police Department, Richard Morris now serves as a reserve deputy constable, United Methodist minister, police chaplain, and a member of the Fort Worth Police Department's peer team and critical incident stress debriefing team. He is also a Ziglar Legacy Certified speaker, trainer, and coach, a tenth degree black belt in karate, and was appointed as the exclusive personal safety coach for Ziglar, Inc. by Tom Ziglar, CEO.

In 2016, Morris started the *Ziglar: Blue Program,* reaching out to law enforcement agencies to train their officers in several Ziglar programs modified specifically for the challenges that law enforcement officers face. Find more information at http://www.richardmorrisseminars.com.

# PREFACE

Let's face it. There's a whole lot of hurt in this world, and some days, it doesn't seem as if things can possibly get better. We wonder, *How could I ever make a difference when I'm just one person?* And, *I have so many problems of my own—how can I possibly change the world for the better when I'm in the middle of my own struggles?* Or, *I just want to change my world—how do I do that?*

I'm here to tell you that, despite how it may appear now, the very challenges that seem to be holding you back from your dream life are signs along your path to living a life of abundance and making your unique positive impact—starting *today*. It doesn't matter what problems you're facing, how much money you have or don't have, how young or old you are, your education level, whether you have a job or you're unemployed, what mistakes you've made in the past—absolutely none of that dictates our ability to get what we want out of life and leave our world in a better state than we found it.

If you have breath in your lungs, you can change the world. It's true! Our present circumstances can change. And the best part is, all the problems you think are weighing you down can actually begin to go away in the process. Isn't that the best news ever?! We don't have to wait for "someday when" to make an impact and improve our lives! We can begin *right now*!

Growing up, I had so much hope for the future. I was full of big ideas and plans I thought would give me the life of my dreams. I felt sure nothing and no one could stop me, no matter what. After over a decade of working multiple jobs, engaging in unhealthy relationships, experiencing unexplained medical issues, going into significant financial debt, managing emotional struggles, and starting over from nothing, I nearly gave up all faith in myself and the hope for a better life. At my lowest point, I felt as if nothing could pull me out of my despair, and I didn't believe I added much value to the world.

A wise person once told me, "The light at the end of the tunnel is self-lit." He reminded me that I needed to focus on what I can do—and those can-dos would guide me out of my seemingly hopeless situation. I've held inside of me what I need to move forward my whole life! My light at the end of the tunnel wasn't going to be faint, I knew. I was determined to blaze—to shine like the sun!

So many things in life can wound us. We can be victims, or we can choose to take ownership of our situation by realizing that we're responsible for our own lives and getting what we want. By choosing a victim mentality, we place all our personal power in the hands of chance. Problems happen to everyone, even when we do our best to avoid them. Challenges are our calls to action!

We will turn it around, we will use it for good! We can take the ugly pain of suffering and use the lessons of our challenges in powerful ways to help others and ourselves. When we grab ahold of the negative things that come our way—when we choose to confront them rather than hide from them—the fear and pain no longer have control over us. We can experience an abundant life by giving to others!

I believe *you* are an incredible force for good—for yourself and the global community. This book is a basic tool to use as you help create the world you want to see, and it's a tangible way to see the difference you're making as you go! When you find yourself feeling discouraged, pick a mission and select your target. By spreading hope and encouragement, we get what we give!

We're individuals, and we're a team! We bring smiles and delight—and we help make life *bright 'n' sunny, sweet as honey*! Let's have some fun as we spread the sunshine!

Welcome to the Sting-Ops Underground!

—Mandy

INTRODUCTION

We can change the world right from where we are today, but we must wake up to the reality of *possibility* and stop convincing ourselves (or allowing others to convince us) that we can't. We can find and create joy in the dance of life, despite our circumstances.

When everything in my life seemed to have unraveled, I felt as if the world was against me—and I acted like a victim of my problems. After what I believed at the time was more than my share of issues, I finally realized that my circumstances were simply a reflection of the mess inside of me. I could only focus on myself and the bad stuff. All I needed to do to change my situation—improve my relationships, repair my finances, clear the inner and outer clutter, and accomplish my goals—was to get really clear with myself *inside*, and everything on the *outside* would take care of itself. I needed to stop getting so wrapped up in the darkness; I needed to elevate my consciousness and think more of others. The solution for everything was my own responsibility. Each of my challenges was a personalized call to take massive action.

That's right: I'm telling you that life's challenges are gifts, opportunities to learn a lesson and move forward! Challenges show us new paths we might otherwise have missed. If it wasn't for the severe contrast—losing everything and suffering the painful consequences of my choices—I wouldn't have recognized the lessons I needed to learn. I wouldn't have been paying close enough attention to see what changes I needed to make!

During my most hopeless times, a gentle buzzing in the breeze began to spark my awakening. I was recovering from a significant injury while also dealing with a broken engagement and some mysterious medical issues. I was unable to work, out of money, and staying with my parents again after a decade on my own. My dog and I went for daily walks as I healed, but I never would have expected that a short rest break on a park bench could shift my thinking—and my future—so drastically.

I was at rock bottom, exhausted from failed efforts to make things right in all the wrong ways. I was ready to give up. With my face buried in tear-filled palms that hot summer day, I felt sure I didn't matter. *There is no way I can make my mark on the world now*, I thought. *It's too late*. My body was soaked in sweat, but a breeze helped keep the mosquitoes off me. I just sat there, elbows digging into my knees as I cried, feeling invisible and worthless until the buzzing drew uncomfortably close.

Unable to ignore the little revving by my ear, I finally looked up. Too tired to continue with my walk and not wanting to provoke the bee, I stayed seated as it floated in midair until it landed next to me, as if to strike up a conversation. I examined its translucent wings and fuzzy torso. Such a delicate little creature. My mind wandered, and I remember seeing a fellow walker swatting at a bee as she adjusted her earbuds. I was so immersed in feeling sorry for myself that I didn't even care that passersby were witnessing my pity party. *No one cares about you either, bee. At least we have this park bench*. The bee stayed beside me until I started walking again, distracted by the day's tasks. As my dog and I returned home, though, I couldn't shake the simple interaction with the little buzzer. In years of sadness and pain, my friends and family couldn't get me out of my funk, yet that tiny bee captivated me. Was it that I'd lost everything and had nothing else to anticipate but the company of a bug? Or was it something else?

Later that night, I attempted, one after another, to start half a dozen movies as a way to soothe my sadness, but none could hold my attention. Instead, I opted for a few online searches—and I somehow ended up researching the honeybee. First, colony collapse disorder came up in my Google search. *Hmmm. I kind of have my own collapse disorder right now, don't I?* Next, pollination facts and quotes from famous scientists about our dependence on bees for our food supply. *One in three bites of food consumed is connected to the bee? No way, not these little honeybees.* Information swarmed around my mind, and I couldn't help but be fascinated—my curiosity only grew as I read more. *How can such a little, seemingly insignificant thing be so vital to our existence? To everyone's? What about me? I feel like nothing. But if a bee can make such a big difference, and it doesn't even try . . . . Am I seeing this clearly? Surely I can bring more to the world than a bee. I have a mind and dreams. Could I ever contribute on this type of global scale?* I knew the answer was yes, but how could it be done? It must have been nearly dawn by the time I fell asleep in the process of learning more about this pollinator.

On my walk the next day, things didn't quite look the same. I wondered if I would see any bumblebees or another friendly honeybee. I noticed how the flowers stretched toward the sun. *The bees go from flower to flower. One flower at a time. One thing at a time. That's how bees make their impact. Flower by flower. Every day. All day.*

I also noticed something new about the faces of the people I passed. A kind smile from a passing stranger carried a new significance. I couldn't help myself from smiling once one had been offered to me on a friendly face. Until then, I'd been feeling alone and invisible, as if I were flying under the radar. My silly grin carried to the next person who passed, and a smile was returned. *Flower by flower. One at a time. One interaction, one smile—it keeps echoing forward.* That little bee became a symbolic driving force for me.

My week continued, and things everywhere seemed off. I saw an alarming number of people walking around apparently oblivious to those around them. Fiddling on their smartphones, playing a game, or scrolling through social media—completely unaware of the people right in front of them who desperately need attention, companionship, and love. Almost as if they were so immersed in a virtual world that they were swatting away actual humans who buzzed too near their personal tech bubble.

Did my winged acquaintance at the park bench wake me up? Why hadn't I been paying attention? Those people—those living, breathing, beautiful souls in front of me—deserved to have human connections in the real world. And I deserved that from others just as much, but I was isolating myself. I wanted to contribute to the world—give of myself to others—but I was afraid. Afraid of being hurt? Not being accepted as I am? Also, I didn't know how to accept kindness from others. I wanted to change the world, but I desperately needed to make changes first in myself.

In a typical working season, a bee's life expectancy is about six weeks. On average during that time, it produces approximately one-tenth of a teaspoon of honey. The honeybee doesn't sleep, and it's vulnerable to many challenges both in and out of its hive.

These complex creatures work diligently to seek out pollen and bring it back to the colony. It's not an easy life by any measure, yet the magnitude of their labor extends far beyond the hive, impacting generations of plants, animals, and people through pollination (alongside their other pollinating-species counterparts). Altogether, they help produce nearly a third of our global food supply. Keep in mind, bees don't set out to change the world. They're just minding their own beeswax (literally!), taking care of their hivemates and home. Their global impact happens as a positive consequence to minding the hive. By taking care of itself and its family, each bee affects goodness for everyone in and outside of the hive. If a little bee can contribute on that scale, just imagine what you and I can accomplish by minding our hives—and by venturing beyond our own hive! Remember how they do it: one flower at a time. How do we change the world? One thing, one interaction, at a time. By taking care of ourselves and those around us—by minding our hives—that's how we can *bee* the change in the world we want to see!

No matter where you're from, what you look like, how much money you possess, or your education or job status—you can make a massive difference in the world. If we each work to improve one thing at a time in our lives, and in the lives of those right in front of us—we can, flower by flower, improve our world. And we don't have to put it off until later! We can start now, in ourselves and in our own neighborhives! It doesn't matter where you are in life, what you have or don't have; it's a basic human need to feel connection, and we can all give and receive that today. We all need caring and kindness—and those too are things we can all give, no matter our current situation. Caring and kindness are a universal language—or maybe we could think of them as the most universally accepted currency.

Did you know that bee venom is used to make medicines? Bee venom is a poison, but when it's medicinally given as a shot, it can help treat nerve pain, multiple sclerosis, rheumatoid arthritis, tendonitis, and muscle conditions. It's also used to help reduce the allergic reaction to bee stings through venom immunotherapy. What I find most interesting about bee-venom therapy is that bee stings can be fatal; yet the very poison that kills can actually be used to improve, even save, lives.

Here's another lesson from our bee friends. If you get stung by one of life's challenges, turn it into something good. Turn the sting into an inoculation, a *blesSTING*! Our problems are a personal call to action. Let's turn those troubles upside down and help someone else in the process. Let's make our own sunshine, and spread it around.

When we reach out to others in the midst of our own pain, we help them—but we also give ourselves a gift. The people we help actually *help us* out of our own slump. Remember that as human beings we all want to help each other; being able to contribute is a key part of who we are, our core purpose! We see the opportunity to help someone and want to act—not because we look down on them; that's just how humans are wired—to love and care for one another. Keep that in mind when someone gives to you! When you receive an act of kindness, a *blesSTING*, pay it forward! When you get stung, pass it on! Changing the world for the better can look different to everyone, but the best thing to remember is that it's all about the little things. Small acts have a huge impact.

We all can be generous, and that generosity doesn't always require money. Share what you have by being your authentic self. Be generous with your time, mental presence, kindness, encouragement, humor, and spirit of fun. Be sincere and uplifting with your words. Make it a goal to cheer up that cranky cashier in the checkout lane. Learn how to become the best listener in the lives of those you know! If you possess a particular skill set, teach someone who'd like to learn from you. Simply being present by consistently "showing up" for someone as his or her own personal cheering section and biggest fan (even if it's not in person) is one of the best examples. Any interaction where you leave someone feeling special, unique, and appreciated is a successful act of generosity.

I want to emphasize the equal importance of committing your own acts of kindness and catching others in an act of generosity to encourage them. When we focus only on doing good, the result is feeling empty and exhausted; the truth is, we're all in this life together. We can't navigate it on our own. Keeping our eyes open to the rest of the world and the good others are doing lifts us up, allows us to accept kindness (and, in turn, give others that great feeling of being able to give), and inspires us to touch the world in other ways we hadn't yet considered. Acknowledging people and the amazing light they bring can help them continue their good work and feel motivated by the realization that they're making a recognizable difference!

Just because we can't always understand the big picture of life, it doesn't mean nothing matters or you don't matter—because *it does* and *you do*. Destroy the notion that you're defective or something is wrong with you. Everything has a purpose, and we're all connected. How can we use the bumps on life's road for good? How can we use our challenges to help ourselves and others along the way?

Problems aren't meant to destroy us; they're our motivation, our personal calls to action. What we feel we're lacking is exactly what we need to give to others. It's in that effort, mastering selflessness in our pain, where our life's purpose and our legacy are born.

How to Use This Book

This book is divided into one hundred sting-ops missions. Some missions are to be completed by a team, while others can be done on your own. Keep in mind that each mission description is simple—an outline, really—so you can make it your own and complete in it the way that best suits your circumstances. You can complete the missions in whichever order you'd like, and even modify them as you go. This isn't about following every single detail to the letter—it's about having fun *beeing* you, and sharing that uniqueness you are with the world to make it a better place.

Each sting-ops mission is followed by a debriefing page to help you explore how it went. Be sure to include as many details as you can right after you complete your mission, when it's still fresh in your mind. This will help you remember the best parts of the sting operation and encourage you to record your ideas for the next time. After you complete your mission and mission debriefing, you can mark it as "MISSION COMPLETE"! If you have the Sting-Ops Tactical Map at home (visit the Sting-Ops Shop at blesSTING.com for more information on tactical gear), you can mark it there as well to display those great *blesSTINGs* you've accomplished in your neighborhive! How wonderful to be able to see part of the difference you're making in the world every day!

Sting-Ops Mission Decoder

Each of your sting-ops missions is organized in the same way so you'll have a good idea of what you need before you begin—much like ingredients listed at the beginning of a recipe. Keep in mind that what's listed isn't all-inclusive. You may find that other helpful tools and hints are required for your mission. Great work on the discovery, sting operative! Now that's ninja vision! Be sure to share your findings with the rest of the Sting-Ops Underground by visiting blesSTING.com and uploading that brilliant stuff! Not only will you have a more impactful sting-ops mission with your own mission target, but you'll be helping other difference-making heroes who can use your genius too!

Here are the other terms you'll encounter in each mission description:

> **SOLO OPS**—sting-ops missions to be completed as an individual

> **TEAM OPS**—sting-ops missions to complete as a group of two or more people

TARGET—the person, place, group, and so on, you choose to direct your sting-ops mission toward (e.g., a neighbor, a service member, community area, etc.)

TIME—the estimated amount of time you'll need to complete the sting-ops mission

COST—the dollar signs indicate the range of what each mission may cost; many require little (if any) money at all!

$ = free to $5

$$ = $5 to $20

$$$ = $20 and up

 MISSION OBJECTIVE—the general overview or goal of the sting-ops mission

 GEAR & PROVISIONS—lists the physical equipment or know-how you'll need to make your mission a success

 PREP STEP—describes a few things to be aware of or do before you begin your mission that will help you prepare

 GO TIME!—the step-by-step process of completing your sting-ops mission

 TACTICAL SUCCESS KEY—helpful tips to help you *go MAD* (make a difference) without *getting mad* if it gets tricky!

Buzzwords

Throughout the book, you'll find some words and terminology made especially for *You: The Sting Operative*. Now that you've joined us in the Sting-Ops Underground, let's define the terms for your reference:

blesSTING—an act of kindness or encouragement completed in the interest of an individual, group, or community's well-being

cyberhiver—a sting operative or neighborhive ninja who is actively on the Internet preparing for or completing sting-ops missions, right from his or her own neighborhive

hive five—long-distance high five from a sting operative, neighborhive ninja, or neighbor hiver!

neighborhive—your neighborhood, backyard, or community (i.e., where you are right now)

neighbor hiver—a person in your neighborhive—friend, family, coworker, classmate, hivemate, or neighbor

sting operation (sting op)—a planned act of kindness/encouragement (or a *blesSTING*) to change the world, right from your own neighborhive

ninja vision—your keen and stealthy observational skills that will allow you to see the opportunities around you to make a difference

sunshine (spread the sunshine)—a pay-it-forward philosophy; also used for acts of kindness and encouragement (or *blesSTING*s)

ninjanuity—your creativity and ingenuity to complete a sting-ops mission or *blesSTING* in your own amazing way; also, the ability to 1) be flexible when things don't go according to plan, and 2) keep it fun, kind, and encouraging anyway!

sting-ops mission target—an individual, group, or community you selected to *sting* with an act of kindness or encouragement through a sting-ops mission

my hive—your home or where you are in your neighborhive; also can be used to reference your mind ("mind the hive")

Sting-Ops Underground—global community of difference-makers both seen and unseen (the anonymous sting operatives and neighborhive ninjas)

Go MAD—acronym for "go make a difference"

Bring the sting!—the winning cheer of sting operatives and neighborhive ninjas to take action—to spread the sunshine through acts of kindness and encouragement (*blesSTING*s, sting-ops missions, etc.) right from their own neighborhive

Get stung. Pass it on.—when you receive an act of kindness or encouragement (or *blesSTING*), pay it forward to someone else in a way that best suits him or her; also, when you face a challenge in life (one of life's stings), choose to give kindness or encouragement to someone else to help him or her and yourself

Sting-Ops Underground

You're an important key to bringing good to the world with each act of kindness and encouragement you do. You're a *blesSTING* operative! What does that mean? It means you're like a ninja next door—an undercover superhero of sorts—making a difference behind the scenes and inspiring others to do the same. Some of the solo-ops missions have you as the target—because practicing kindness with yourself is extremely important too! Remember, it's not your job to save the world, but when we all work together to spread the sunshine, the world will absolutely be changed for the better, right from our own neighborhives.

What if the mission doesn't go according to plan? That's OK! The most important thing is to keep a genuinely caring and giving attitude, and do your best to brighten someone's day. This is a learning experience, and the only thing that would be wrong is if your motive is self-serving. Do your best and let the universe take care of the rest. Not everyone knows how to accept kindness and generosity, you and me included. It's all good—keep giving, keep growing, keep going!

Honoring the Underground

Why is it so important that some acts of kindness are anonymous? Many people have a hard time accepting kindness due to bad past experiences or other barriers, so being "undercover" will help your sting ops have the maximum impact. By completing as many ops as you're able without your target knowing who they've been *blesSTUNG* by will help them build back their faith and trust in people, and also prompt them to pay it forward: they get stung and then pass it on. This is how we spread the sunshine across the globe!

This book contains one hundred ways to change the world from your own neighborhive—but it's only a beginning! Use the provided templates to add your own amazing mission ideas, and please feel free to share them with the Sting-Ops Underground difference-making community by visiting blesSTING.com.

Have fun as you spread the sunshine, neighborhive ninja! Keep *beeing* your wonderful self as you change the world for the better, one *blesSTING* at a time!

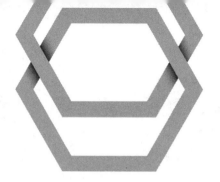

A SINGLE ACTION CAN SPARK LIMITLESS
OPPORTUNITIES FOR WORLD CHANGE.

BEGIN.

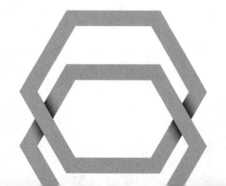

100 TACTICS TO CHANGE THE WORLD

(Right from Your Own Neighborhive!)
One blesSTING at a time!

1. Send a handwritten card to a veteran or active serviceperson.

2. Practice gratitude every day.

3. "Adopt" a local beehive.

4. Gather food to donate to a local food shelf.

5. Learn about a cause you want to support and share that knowledge.

6. Shop at local farmers' markets.

7. Leave every place you go better than you found it.

8. Support a local entrepreneur.

9. Put away your mobile device and smile at or talk to someone you don't already know.

10. Drive less, walk more.

11. Thank your cashier for his or her excellent work.

12. Be *present* in each moment.

13. Use social media to spread encouragement, good news, and love.

14. Surprise the family of a deployed soldier with a treat.

15. Anonymously pay for a stranger's meal at a restaurant as you leave.

16. Compost at home and at work.

17. Mentor kids or young adults.

18. Tell a good, clean joke.

19. Hand out cold drinks to outdoor workers on a hot day.

20. Write a letter to the boss of someone you've noticed doing excellent, standout work.

21. Make a pollinator hydration station for bees and butterflies.

22. Look yourself in the eye every morning and say: "It's a new day. I'm adding light and goodness to everyone I meet today!"

23. Offer a free night of childcare to a friend or neighbor hiver around the holiday season.

24. Hold the door open for others.

25. Prepare a meal for a grieving family.

26. Eat local, and eat organic whenever possible.

27. Collect cold-weather gear for the homeless in your community.

28. Learn something by listening to others first before speaking.

29. Read to kids.

30. Recognize others' random acts of kindness and encouragement.

31. More living potted plants at home and at work, fewer artificial air fresheners!

32. Plan a family game night.

33. Be helpful to someone who is moving.

34. Donate teaching supplies to a local classroom.

35. Carpool!

36. Brainstorm ways to make a difference with local students.

37. Clean and declutter your house, and then donate what you aren't using anymore.

38. Pick up trash.

39. "Adopt" a grandparent.

40. Wash someone's car on a sunny day.

41. Read more.

42. Conserve water and energy at home and at the office.

43. Teach a community-education class.

44. Invite a neighbor hiver over for dinner.

45. Make a wall of sunshine to celebrate acts of kindness and encouragement.

46. Be curious, ask questions, and seek to understand more in conversations.

47. Organize a community cleanup day with your neighbors.

48. Anonymously surprise a hardworking couple with a gift card for a date night.

49. Pack more nutritious lunches.

50. Grow bee-friendly plants and flowers in your yard.

51. Call your grandparent, aunt, uncle, or parent to share a memory and catch up.

52. Share books and magazines in your neighborhive.

53. Forgive often.

54. Spark an ongoing conversation about opportunities to improve your neighborhive.

55. Help prepare a young person for a career by helping him or her craft a résumé.

56. Compliment a child on his or her unique contribution to the world.

57. Feed the birds.

58. Volunteer more!

59. Help someone get home who can't on his or her own.

60. Treat your mail carrier.

61. Speak up with constructive ideas and solutions.

62. Use your skills to help fix something for a neighbor.

63. Support local kids' sports leagues, art programs, and activities.

64. Join a community-supported agriculture (CSA) program in your area.

65. Take care of you.

66. Anonymously do yard work or shovel snow from your neighbor hiver's sidewalk or driveway while he or she is out.

67. Encourage someone who is pursuing a goal.

68. Pay for the person behind you at the drive-through.

69. Filter your water at home and use a reusable bottle.

70. Tuck a five-dollar bill into a library book before returning it.

71. *Bee* a buddy to neighborhive kids.

72. Give new or gently used toys to a local women's shelter.

73. Practice kindness toward a homeless person.

74. Help someone in your neighborhive who may need assistance with grocery shopping and unpacking their purchases at home.

75. Minimize extra driving and air pollution by planning out your errands in advance.

76. Participate in something you've never done to make new friends.

77. Buy only what you need; don't waste.

78. Get a pen pal and send some long-distance sunshine. :-)

79. Learn another language, and then practice with someone who speaks it as a first language.

80. Recycle and upcycle.

81. Uplift and celebrate differences and uncommon abilities.

82. Enjoy more meatless meals with your family on a regular basis.

83. Start a community garden.

84. Organize family volunteering opportunities in addition to entertainment activities like movies or theme parks.

85. Anonymously pay for someone's groceries.

86. Send letters of encouragement.

87. Bring a beverage to your neighborhive garbage-removal team.

88. Cultivate a pollinator garden in the community.

89. Shut off social media for a week and go meet people in your community.

90. Donate stuffed animals for kids who have to ride in an ambulance or police car.

91. Volunteer to read to or spend time with residents of a nursing home or hospice.

92. Help the elderly learn how to connect to friends and family using the Internet.

93. Help a local farmer with chores for a day.

94. Organize a neighborhood outdoor food and music or movie night.

95. *blesSTING* someone with a sunny note.

96. Surprise your neighbors with a homemade treat.

97. Explore new dishes with foods and flavors you've never tasted before.

98. Enjoy days without your cell phone, computer, and TV.

99. Help make someone's dream (or holiday wish!) come true.

100. Learn more about sustainable agriculture and how you can help your community.

SPREAD THE SUNSHINE!

SEND A HANDWRITTEN CARD TO A VETERAN OR ACTIVE SERVICEPERSON
solo op or team op

1

TARGET: Veteran or active serviceperson (e.g., military, community leader, or local volunteer)

TIME: 00:10+

COST: $

 MISSION OBJECTIVE:

Send a handwritten card to bring a little sunshine to a veteran or active serviceperson.

GEAR & PROVISIONS:

- Contact information/mailing address
- Note cards or stationery and postage stamps

☑ PREP STEP:

Think about those making sacrifices in service to others, consider what you want to say to thank them. Write it down and send them some sunshine!

🕐 GO TIME!

1. Select your mission target: the card recipient.
2. Write a thoughtful and genuine note.
3. Send it off with some sunshine and positive energy!

📍 TACTICAL SUCCESS KEY:

Your note can be whatever length feels natural to you. Stay focused on thanking and cheering on your mission target. As long as you use your authentic voice and speak from your heart, your mission will be a success. You rock!

MY NEIGHBORHIVE MISSION DEBRIEFING
mission completion date

how do you feel after completing the sting operation?

what did you notice afterwards?
- about your mission target
- yourself/team
- surroundings/neighborhive

what will you want to do again with this mission to make your target feel special/that you made a difference?

what ideas do you have for your next sting ops mission?

PRACTICE GRATITUDE EVERY DAY

solo op or team op

2

TARGET: You and others
TIME: 00:05+
COST: $

🎯 MISSION OBJECTIVE:

Open your eyes to the sunshine in your life by practicing gratitude every day.

⚙️ GEAR & PROVISIONS:

- Attitude of gratitude
- List of things to be grateful for
- Thank-you cards
- Postage stamps

☑️ PREP STEP:

Look around you—pictures of the people you hold dear, material possessions—there are so many things to be grateful for, even when it just seems like another day vertical!

🕐 GO TIME!

1. Keep a running list of "Things I Am Grateful For" to post at home, work, or school.

2. Make it a personal challenge each day or week to add one more item to your gratitude list.

3. Use thank-you cards to express your gratitude to others for their roles in your life, and do your best to run out of your stationery before each month's end! How grateful can you be?

4. Say thank you to people as they add value to your life in real time! Or pick up a phone to give them a surprise call!

🔑 TACTICAL SUCCESS KEY:

Feel the good, kindness, and love in your life each day, and then spread it around! Positive energy brings great things into your life! Thank you for being you, and for your attitude of gratitude in a world that sometimes forgets how good we truly have it!

MY NEIGHBORHIVE MISSION DEBRIEFING
mission completion date
....

how do you feel after completing the sting operation?

....

....

....

what did you notice afterwards?
- about your mission target
- yourself/team
- surroundings/neighborhive

....

....

....

what will you want to do again with this mission to make your target feel special/that you made a difference?

....

....

....

what ideas do you have for your next sting ops mission?

....

....

....

"ADOPT" A LOCAL BEEHIVE

3

solo op or team op

TARGET: Local bee population
TIME: 01:00+
COST: $$-$$$

MISSION OBJECTIVE:

Partner with a local beekeeper to help support the bee population while also learning a bit about beekeeping.

GEAR & PROVISIONS:

- "How can I help?" spirit of learning and giving
- The cooperation of a local beekeeper

PREP STEP:

Spend a little time looking up local bee programs and beekeepers. Think about how you want to help and what you want to learn. Then call them with your questions to see which one will be the best fit for you.

GO TIME!

1. Inquire about local beekeeping activities, and seek out a place where you can volunteer.

2. Learn about and help foster your local bee population.

3. Enjoy your local honey crop!

TACTICAL SUCCESS KEY:

Keep in mind that not all beekeeping operations are able to accommodate on-site visitors due to local regulations or their own policies. Many areas have existing programs for a hands-on experience, or off-site learning opportunities. See what's available in your neighborhive, and keep up the great attitude. *Go, do, bee!*

MY NEIGHBORHIVE MISSION DEBRIEFING
mission completion date
....

how do you feel after completing the sting operation?

....

....

what did you notice afterwards?
- about your mission target
- yourself/team
- surroundings/neighborhive

....

....

....

what will you want to do again with this mission to make your target feel special/that you made a difference?

....

....

what ideas do you have for your next sting ops mission?

....

....

....

GATHER FOOD TO DONATE TO LOCAL FOOD SHELF

team op

4

TARGET: Neighbor hivers experiencing tough times

TIME: 01:00+

COST: $-$$$

 MISSION OBJECTIVE:

Help nourish your neighbor hivers in need by leading a donation drive for your local food shelf.

GEAR & PROVISIONS:

- Your food-drive team!
- Local organization(s) to partner with
- Date and time to gather donations and deliver them to the food shelf
- Lots of caring, love, and respect for your neighbor hivers every step of the way

PREP STEP:

Keep your winning, can-do attitude and willingness to serve others at the forefront of your mind. We're a community—a hive—and every bee can use a helping hand from time to time.

GO TIME!

1. Spread the word that you're stocking the local food shelf! Let people know what you need (and if there are any special guidelines, etc.).

2. *Bee* buzzed about your cause! Set goals and stretch to exceed them. You're making a huge difference for families in need!

3. Gather donations and deliver them to food shelf.

TACTICAL SUCCESS KEY:

Put yourself in someone else's shoes. It isn't easy to ask for help, especially when it comes to basic needs. We're in this life together, and it's a privilege to help out our fellow neighbor hivers. Remember to be kind and considerate in your efforts, and focus on nourishing and shoring up the dignity of those who are going through difficult times. Spread that sunshine!

MY NEIGHBORHIVE MISSION DEBRIEFING
mission completion date
....

how do you feel after completing the sting operation?

....

....

....

what did you notice afterwards?
- about your mission target
- yourself/team
- surroundings/neighborhive

....

....

what will you want to do again with this mission to make your target feel special/that you made a difference?

....

....

....

what ideas do you have for your next sting ops mission?

....

....

....

LEARN ABOUT A CAUSE YOU WANT TO SUPPORT AND SHARE THAT KNOWLEDGE
solo op

5

TARGET: You
TIME: 00:30+
COST: $

🎯 MISSION OBJECTIVE:
Expand your horizons and capacity to help by learning about a cause and how you can increase awareness about it.

⚙️ GEAR & PROVISIONS:
- Willingness to learn and help others
- Area of interest or a special cause
- Access to the Internet or a public library
- Local organization contact

☑️ PREP STEP:
Think about what tugs at your heart. What causes inspire you to help?

🕐 GO TIME!
1. Research different causes that interest you.
2. Connect with a local organization or people who can introduce you to specific opportunities to help.
3. Keep up that wonderful attitude of learning and volunteer to add value where and when you're able.

🔑 TACTICAL SUCCESS KEY:
Keep an open mind. Feed your appetite for knowledge, and share your heart to help others. We're all on this journey together, and there are many different causes that can benefit from your unique skills and energy. You have so much to give to the world by just *beeing you*!

MY NEIGHBORHIVE MISSION DEBRIEFING
mission completion date
....

how do you feel after completing the sting operation?

....

....

....

what did you notice afterwards?
- about your mission target
- yourself/team
- surroundings/neighborhive

....

....

....

what will you want to do again with this mission to make your target feel special/that you made a difference?

....

....

....

what ideas do you have for your next sting ops mission?

....

....

....

SHOP AT LOCAL FARMERS' MARKETS

6

solo op or team op

TARGET: Area farmers, you
TIME: 00:30+
COST: $-$$$

MISSION OBJECTIVE:

Enjoy fresher food and support area growers by shopping at local farmers' markets.

GEAR & PROVISIONS:

- Research on local community-supported agriculture (CSA) programs
- Online resources to find farmers' market locations and schedules
- In-season schedule for crops to strategize your shopping
- An interest in getting to know your local farmer

PREP STEP:

Ask your friends and neighbor hivers about their favorite ways to access locally sourced food. Have fun trying new things from your neighborhive growers!

GO TIME!

1. Read the wealth of agricultural information online and in books, and ask local farmers lots of questions!

2. Shop at farmers' markets as frequently as possible.

3. Find out where your grocery store's produce is sourced to make educated decisions about what you're feeding yourself and your family.

TACTICAL SUCCESS KEY:

Explore your area farmers' markets with a friend. Discover which ones you like the best for specific items so you can help each other save time and money as you make your stops.

MY NEIGHBORHIVE MISSION DEBRIEFING
mission completion date ....

how do you feel after completing the sting operation?

....

....

....

what did you notice afterwards?
- about your mission target
- yourself/team
- surroundings/neighborhive

....

what will you want to do again with this mission to make your target feel special/that you made a difference?

....

....

....

what ideas do you have for your next sting ops mission?

....

....

....

LEAVE EVERY PLACE YOU GO BETTER THAN YOU FOUND IT

solo op or team op

7

TARGET: Your home and neighborhive

TIME: 00:05+

COST: $

🎯 MISSION OBJECTIVE:

Keep your neighborhive pleasant by making an effort to leave the places you go a little (or maybe a lot!) better than you found them.

⚙️ GEAR & PROVISIONS:

- Winning "add value where you are" attitude!
- Awareness of surroundings

☑️ PREP STEP:

Clean up and improve your surroundings as you go. It's not so daunting when done in little bits! Practice gratitude on the go: What do you appreciate in your neighborhive? What would you like to do to improve it? How do you think others would like to see the community improve?

🕐 GO TIME!

1. Stay aware.

2. Be mindful of others and your surroundings. Stay positive with your thoughts and words.

3. Be your awesome ninja self, improving things around you as you go. They'll all wonder, "How did it suddenly get better?" (Because of you!)

🔑 TACTICAL SUCCESS KEY:

You don't need to turn every place into a showplace—just focus on the little things, incremental improvements, leaving few or no footprints. When everyone does a little extra, everything changes massively for the better. And it doesn't take much effort at all. You rock!

MY NEIGHBORHIVE MISSION DEBRIEFING
mission completion date
....

how do you feel after completing the sting operation?

....

....

....

what did you notice afterwards?
- about your mission target
- yourself/team
- surroundings/neighborhive

....

....

....

....

what will you want to do again with this mission to make your target feel special/that you made a difference?

....

....

....

what ideas do you have for your next sting ops mission?

....

....

....

SUPPORT A LOCAL ENTREPRENEUR

solo op or team op

8

TARGET: Local small-business owner
TIME: 00:30+
COST: $-$$$

🎯 MISSION OBJECTIVE:

Demonstrate your support for a local small business by buying its goods or services, or investing in it if you have the desire and means to do so.

⚙️ GEAR & PROVISIONS:

- Knowledge of local businesses
- Shopping list (if you're buying their goods)
- Your questions for the owner (if you're looking to invest)
- A friendly smile and a "thanks for doing business in our community" attitude

☑️ PREP STEP:

Check out your local chamber of commerce website or online directory to find out more about the local folks doing business in your neighborhive.

🕐 GO TIME!

1. Learn about the local businesses in your neighborhive.

2. Seek out opportunities to support them by buying their goods or services whenever you can.

3. If you're in a position to make investments, consult with your financial professional about the details when small-business investment opportunities arise.

🔑 TACTICAL SUCCESS KEY:

Do your homework, and support the businesses that make sense to you. Sometimes shopping at national chains fits your needs, while in other cases you can get a great experience supporting your neighborhive business owners. Consult with your licensed financial professional when considering investment opportunities, and remember to have fun as you learn and connect with your community's small-business leaders.

MY NEIGHBORHIVE MISSION DEBRIEFING
mission completion date ....

how do you feel after completing the sting operation?

....

....

....

what did you notice afterwards?
- about your mission target
- yourself/team
- surroundings/neighborhive

....

what will you want to do again with this mission to make your target feel special/that you made a difference?

....

....

....

what ideas do you have for your next sting ops mission?

....

....

....

PUT AWAY YOUR MOBILE DEVICE TO SMILE AT OR TALK TO SOMEONE YOU DON'T ALREADY KNOW
solo op

9

TARGET: Someone you haven't spoken to yet

TIME: 00:05

COST: $

MISSION OBJECTIVE:

Meet a new friend, learn something about him or her, bring sunshine and joy to his or her day!

GEAR & PROVISIONS:

- Smile!
- (Not your smartphone or mobile device!)
- A few questions to help you learn about your new friend

PREP STEP:

Put away your phone and other mobile devices. Keep in mind what it feels like when others are distracted and not fully present during a conversation. Focus on giving your target your full presence, and how to leave him or her feeling acknowledged, appreciated, and special.

GO TIME!

1. Make eye contact and smile! :-)
2. Ask a simple question to spark conversation. Show interest in your new acquaintance as a person.
3. Wish him or her a great day!

TACTICAL SUCCESS KEY:

It's all about spreading the sunshine from where you are, so you don't need to plan an extra trip outside of your normal routine to make it happen. Learn to see opportunities unfold before you each day, and then take action. The best thing is to have a natural interaction (on the way to school or work, at a store, or in checkout line, etc.). Be authentic and genuine—*bee* you!

MY NEIGHBORHIVE MISSION DEBRIEFING
mission completion date ....

how do you feel after completing the sting operation?

....

....

....

what did you notice afterwards?
  • about your mission target
  • yourself/team
  • surroundings/neighborhive

....

what will you want to do again with this mission to make your target feel special/that you made a difference?

....

....

....

what ideas do you have for your next sting ops mission?

....

....

....

DRIVE LESS, WALK MORE

solo op or team op

10

TARGET: You and others
TIME: Varies, ongoing
COST: $

MISSION OBJECTIVE:
Get your rear in gear, and encourage others to join you!

GEAR & PROVISIONS:
- Good walking shoes
- Walking buddy
- Outdoor gear for all weather conditions

PREP STEP:
Plan your required driving trips to reduce unnecessary dashboard time—then get out to enjoy that fresh air and sunshine whenever you can!

GO TIME!
1. Plan your driving trips carefully to minimize them as much as possible.
2. Find a walking buddy to keep it fun!
3. Track your steps with a pedometer, and then challenge yourself to go farther each day!

TACTICAL SUCCESS KEY:
Keep it fun! Enjoy the outdoors—relish your mobility and taking time for yourself (or spending time with a walking buddy). Ninjas have gotta stay fit to keep their sting ops going strong!

MY NEIGHBORHIVE MISSION DEBRIEFING
mission completion date ....

how do you feel after completing the sting operation?

....

....

....

what did you notice afterwards?

- about your mission target
- yourself/team
- surroundings/neighborhive

....

....

....

what will you want to do again with this mission to make your target feel special/that you made a difference?

....

....

....

what ideas do you have for your next sting ops mission?

....

....

....

THANK YOUR CASHIER FOR HIS OR HER EXCELLENT WORK

solo op

11

TARGET: Neighborhive cashier or store associate

TIME: 00:03

COST: $

MISSION OBJECTIVE:

Brighten the day of your neighborhive cashier or store associate by recognizing a job well done!

GEAR & PROVISIONS:

- Smile!
- Ninja vision to catch someone doing his or her job with excellence!

PREP STEP:

These folks are working very hard at their jobs. Be genuine and authentic. Let the conversation be natural, uplifting, and brief (because they're still at work).

GO TIME!

1. Begin with an attitude of "how can I brighten this person's day?"

2. Smile, and start by acknowledging their friendliness, smile, customer-service skills, speed of service, and so on.

3. Say thank you, and wish your target an excellent day!

TACTICAL SUCCESS KEY:

Keep in mind that neighborhive retail workers are on the job and may not have much time to chat. Spread the sunshine as you continue your errands, and leave the people you interact with feeling brighter than you found them! Go, ninja, go!

MY NEIGHBORHIVE MISSION DEBRIEFING
mission completion date ....

how do you feel after completing the sting operation?

....

....

what did you notice afterwards?
- about your mission target
- yourself/team
- surroundings/neighborhive

what will you want to do again with this mission to make your target feel special/that you made a difference?

....

....

what ideas do you have for your next sting ops mission?

....

....

BE PRESENT IN EACH MOMENT

solo op

TARGET: You and others
TIME: Daily
COST: $

🎯 MISSION OBJECTIVE:

Stay an active participant in your daily life by being fully engaged.

⚙️ GEAR & PROVISIONS:

- Willingness to work on improving your focus and clarity

- An ongoing, conscious choice to stay in the now

☑️ PREP STEP:

Tell yourself: "I choose to be present in my own life by being focused on the people and tasks right in front of me."

🕐 GO TIME!

1. Be present with others: Pay attention to what people are saying, and process it. Do your best to not think so much about how you'll respond or other things you need to do later.

2. Be present with yourself: Gift yourself with the time you deserve to unplug from everything else and have quality time alone.

3. Be present with the tasks at hand: Embrace the art of focus and single-tasking. Choose one and get it done.

📍 TACTICAL SUCCESS KEY:

Every day—every moment—is an opportunity to give yourself the presence of mind you need to give others the presence they want from you. Without true presence, the task at hand really isn't worthwhile. And when we aren't giving the people around us our full attention, they're getting the message that they're not worthwhile either. When we divide our attention among too many tasks or too many people, we're robbing others (and ourselves) of having joy as our best selves living in the *now*.

MY NEIGHBORHIVE MISSION DEBRIEFING
mission completion date ....

how do you feel after completing the sting operation?

....

....

what did you notice afterwards?
- about your mission target
- yourself/team
- surroundings/neighborhive

....

what will you want to do again with this mission to make your target feel special/that you made a difference?

....

....

....

what ideas do you have for your next sting ops mission?

....

....

....

USE SOCIAL MEDIA TO SPREAD ENCOURAGEMENT, GOOD NEWS, AND LOVE
solo op

13

TARGET: Cyberhivers
TIME: 00:05
COST: $

MISSION OBJECTIVE:
Post positive messages on your social-media feeds that aim to encourage and support your digital community. Avoid contributing to gossip or negative messages.

GEAR & PROVISIONS:

- Your winning attitude to encourage others
- Social-media access

PREP STEP:
It's all about the little things. Don't overthink it. Keep it simple—and if you're lacking your own inspiration at the moment, share someone else's! Yes!

GO TIME!
1. Keep your focus on encouraging others.

2. Select wisely the pictures and words you share. Does your post represent positive, good things?

3. Share the sunshine! Celebrate others who do the same!

TACTICAL SUCCESS KEY:
Not everyone is about helping to make lives bright 'n' sunny, sweet as honey—but you're doing the right thing by taking the high road (or the *hiveroad*)! When others are unkind, don't allow them to steal your sunshine. Keep sharing great energy, and good things will come back to you too!

MY NEIGHBORHIVE MISSION DEBRIEFING
mission completion date
....

how do you feel after completing the sting operation?

....

....

what did you notice afterwards?
- about your mission target
- yourself/team
- surroundings/neighborhive

....

....

....

what will you want to do again with this mission to make your target feel special/that you made a difference?

....

....

....

what ideas do you have for your next sting ops mission?

....

....

....

SURPRISE THE FAMILY OF A DEPLOYED SOLDIER WITH A TREAT

team op

14

TARGET: A family with a soldier on deployment

TIME: 00:35+

COST: $-$$$

MISSION OBJECTIVE:

Bring a little sunshine into the day of family waiting for their soldier to return home.

GEAR & PROVISIONS:

- Giving attitude
- A source to help you find out what the family could use or what they would appreciate
- Resources that will help you fulfill that specific want or need

PREP STEP:

Do a little behind-the-scenes ninja work to find out what will really bless this family and how you can help them in a meaningful way.

GO TIME!

1. Identify what you can do to surprise and delight your target family.

2. Gather the appropriate resources—but keep it under wraps!

3. Spread the sunshine by bringing that surprise to life!

TACTICAL SUCCESS KEY:

The best surprises happen when no one sees it coming! I know you're excited, but keep it a secret until the surprise is ready to be revealed!

MY NEIGHBORHIVE MISSION DEBRIEFING
mission completion date ....

how do you feel after completing the sting operation?

....

....

....

what did you notice afterwards?
- about your mission target
- yourself/team
- surroundings/neighborhive

....

....

what will you want to do again with this mission to make your target feel special/that you made a difference?

....

....

....

what ideas do you have for your next sting ops mission?

....

....

....

ANONYMOUSLY PAY FOR A STRANGER'S MEAL AT A RESTAURANT AS YOU LEAVE
solo op or team op

15

TARGET: Unsuspecting diner

TIME: 00:05

COST: $$-$$$

MISSION OBJECTIVE:
Cover the tab for a stranger's meal at a restaurant—anonymously.

GEAR & PROVISIONS:
- Positive energy!
- Gift card for the restaurant

PREP STEP:
Purchase a gift card to the restaurant as you pay your bill—or buy one in advance of your visit. To remain undetected by your sting-ops target, give the gift card to a server or host and enlist his or her help.

GO TIME!
1. Purchase a gift card to the restaurant.
2. Quietly ask the server or host to use it for the diner across the way.
3. Keep the op under wraps!

TACTICAL SUCCESS KEY:
Keep this sting-ops mission anonymous! You're a meal ninja, spreading sunshine at a restaurant near you!

MY NEIGHBORHIVE MISSION DEBRIEFING
mission completion date
....

how do you feel after completing the sting operation?

....

....

what did you notice afterwards?
- about your mission target
- yourself/team
- surroundings/neighborhive

....

....

....

....

what will you want to do again with this mission to make your target feel special/that you made a difference?

....

....

....

what ideas do you have for your next sting ops mission?

....

....

....

COMPOST AT HOME AND AT WORK

16

solo op or team op

TARGET: Your home and workplace
TIME: Ongoing, varies
COST: $

🎯 MISSION OBJECTIVE:

Manage your waste responsibly by composting at home and at work!

⚙️ GEAR & PROVISIONS:

- List of what's compostable and what isn't
- Composting receptacle
- Plan for compost materials when the containers are full

☑️ PREP STEP:

Do your homework so you'll know what can be composted, what can't, and how and where to use your collected compost materials.

🕐 GO TIME!

1. Compost as you go at home and at work.

2. Empty compost receptacles as they fill; transport the work compost home.

3. Use compost for your home garden and share it with your fellow neighbor hivers.

🔑 TACTICAL SUCCESS KEY:

There are different ways to compost—depending on what you consume, the climate where you live, your plans for how to use the compost, and other factors. Visit your local garden center and do some research online to learn from professionals how you can best compost, and then enjoy watching your garden flourish!

MY NEIGHBORHIVE MISSION DEBRIEFING
mission completion date ....

how do you feel after completing the sting operation?

....

....

....

what did you notice afterwards?
- about your mission target
- yourself/team
- surroundings/neighborhive

....

what will you want to do again with this mission to make your target feel special/that
you made a difference?

....

....

....

what ideas do you have for your next sting ops mission?

....

....

....

TARGET: Kids and young adults in your community

TIME: Varies, ongoing

COST: $

MISSION OBJECTIVE:

Bee a mentor to someone in your area to encourage and help him or her grow!

GEAR & PROVISIONS:

- Consistent time to volunteer or be available
- Partnership with a local organization

PREP STEP:

Get in touch with a local organization to express your interest in volunteering for a mentorship program. Think about what area or skill set you might want to focus on.

GO TIME!

1. Connect with community organizations.

2. Set aside time for volunteering as a mentor.

3. Follow through with your time commitment and focus on how you can best support and cheer on your mentee.

TACTICAL SUCCESS KEY:

Decide in advance how much time you're willing to devote to this type of volunteering and if you wish to focus on a specific area of development or skill set in your mentoring. Some programs keep participants with the same mentor for an extended time, while others change it up each time you volunteer. Ask good questions when doing your research, and have a great time as a mentor and leader in a young person's life!

MY NEIGHBORHIVE MISSION DEBRIEFING
mission completion date ....

how do you feel after completing the sting operation?

....

....

what did you notice afterwards?
* about your mission target ....
* yourself/team ....
* surroundings/neighborhive ....

....

what will you want to do again with this mission to make your target feel special/that you made a difference?

....

....

what ideas do you have for your next sting ops mission?

....

....

TELL A GOOD, CLEAN JOKE

solo op or team op

18

TARGET: You and everyone around you

TIME: 00:05

COST: $

MISSION OBJECTIVE:

Spread the fun and laughter around by sharing a good, clean joke. You'll bring smiles and laughter to the day!

GEAR & PROVISIONS:

- Lighthearted attitude and spirit of fun
- A handful of inoffensive jokes or humorous anecdotes
- A group of people you enjoy being around

☑ PREP STEP:

Stay positive, and keep it clean and uplifting. We can all use more laughter and fun in our lives!

🕑 GO TIME!

Keep a playful approach without tearing down others or making someone the butt of a joke. If you have a hard time coming up with jokes on your own, try an online search or find comedy-inspired books at the library. This will help to get you warmed up to your own unique style.

TACTICAL SUCCESS KEY:

Don't overthink it. Everyone has a different approach to humor, and you can't win them all! Have fun with yourself, and don't take it personally if a punch line ends up backward—sometimes the best joke is one that's misstated. It's all good!

MY NEIGHBORHIVE MISSION DEBRIEFING
mission completion date ....

how do you feel after completing the sting operation?

....

....

....

what did you notice afterwards?
- about your mission target
- yourself/team
- surroundings/neighborhive

....

....

....

what will you want to do again with this mission to make your target feel special/that you made a difference?

....

....

....

what ideas do you have for your next sting ops mission?

....

....

....

HAND OUT COLD DRINKS TO OUTDOOR WORKERS ON A HOT DAY

19

solo op or team op

TARGET: Outdoor neighborhive workers

TIME: 00:05

COST: $

MISSION OBJECTIVE:
Deliver refreshing cold beverages to outdoor workers on a hot day.

GEAR & PROVISIONS:
- Smile!
- Beverage(s)

PREP STEP:
These folks are working very hard in tough conditions. A friendly smile and pleasant attitude can brighten their day.

GO TIME!
1. Prepare your winning attitude, smile, and beverages.
2. Deliver.

TACTICAL SUCCESS KEY:
Keep in mind that outdoor neighborhive workers are on the job, sometimes on a very tight time line (without extra time to chat), and may not be able to accept your act of kindness for reasons they don't control (company policy, local regulations, etc.). This mission is about spreading the sunshine, so wish them a great day even if they decline. Then continue having a fabulous day yourself!

MY NEIGHBORHIVE MISSION DEBRIEFING
mission completion date ....

how do you feel after completing the sting operation?

....

....

....

what did you notice afterwards?
- about your mission target
- yourself/team
- surroundings/neighborhive

....

....

what will you want to do again with this mission to make your target feel special/that you made a difference?

....

....

....

what ideas do you have for your next sting ops mission?

....

....

....

WRITE A LETTER TO THE BOSS OF SOMEONE YOU'VE NOTICED DOING EXCELLENT, STANDOUT WORK
solo op or team op

20

TARGET: Someone you notice doing a great job

TIME: 00:10+

COST: $

MISSION OBJECTIVE:
Written acknowledgment of a job well done! Write a note to the boss or supervisor of someone you see doing an excellent job, someone who stands out among the rest.

GEAR & PROVISIONS:
- E-mail access or stationery and postage
- Contact information for the person's employer
- Name of the exemplary employee
- Sincere, authentic, and specific feedback

PREP STEP:
Consider the challenges your target may face daily in his or her line of work. Think about how his or her unique ability shines through the job's duties, and find a way to acknowledge that in an uplifting way.

GO TIME!
1. Access your most encouraging mind-set.
2. Recall specific details about how this person wowed you.
3. Write an e-mail or letter to your target's boss.
4. Send or deliver the note.

TACTICAL SUCCESS KEY:
Keep your praise specific, professional, concise, and direct. Be genuine without exaggerating, and have fun as you spread the sunshine! Everyone wants to get good feedback on a job well done!

MY NEIGHBORHIVE MISSION DEBRIEFING
mission completion date
....

how do you feel after completing the sting operation?

....

....

....

what did you notice afterwards?
- about your mission target
- yourself/team
- surroundings/neighborhive

....

what will you want to do again with this mission to make your target feel special/that you made a difference?

....

....

....

what ideas do you have for your next sting ops mission?

....

....

....

MAKE A POLLINATOR HYDRATION STATION FOR BEES AND BUTTERFLIES
solo op or team op

21

TARGET: Pollinators in your neighborhive

TIME: 00:30+

COST: $$-$$$

MISSION OBJECTIVE:

Add a pollinator station to your yard so bees and butterflies have a place to hydrate in the midst of all their hard work.

GEAR & PROVISIONS:

- Online resources for plans to make a bee break station
- Clean water
- Dish and grate from your local hardware store
- Choice location in your yard for a bee break station

PREP STEP:

After finding plans online, visit your local hardware store to gather materials for your pollinator rest stop.

GO TIME!

1. Pick a do-it-yourself pollinator station plan.
2. Buy supplies, and assemble them according to your chosen plan.
3. Fill the station with water and place it in your yard for pollinators to hydrate throughout the day.

TACTICAL SUCCESS KEY:

This is a simple project that you can do on your own or with others. Be sure to use clean water. This isn't a birdbath; the bees and pollinators need fresh water to hydrate in between flower stops. Refill it often, being especially attentive to keep it filled when temperatures rise. Hydrated bees are happy bees!

MY NEIGHBORHIVE MISSION DEBRIEFING
mission completion date ....

how do you feel after completing the sting operation?
....
....
....

what did you notice afterwards?
- about your mission target   ....
- yourself/team   ....
- surroundings/neighborhive   ....
....

what will you want to do again with this mission to make your target feel special/that you made a difference?
....
....
....

what ideas do you have for your next sting ops mission?
....
....
....

LOOK YOURSELF IN THE EYE EVERY MORNING AND SAY: "IT'S A NEW DAY. I'M ADDING LIGHT AND GOODNESS TO EVERYONE I MEET TODAY!"

22

solo op

TARGET: You
TIME: 00:02+
COST: $

MISSION OBJECTIVE:
Mind the hive, and start the day off right with some positive self-talk, you sunshine-making ninja!

GEAR & PROVISIONS:
- Great attitude
- A power phrase you use to get in your awesome zone for the day (e.g., "It's going to be a great day!")

PREP STEP:
We know words are a powerful force, but sometimes we forget to be mindful of how we speak to ourselves. Remember that words can be used to create good or bad, so choose your words wisely—especially the ones you say to yourself!

GO TIME!
Wake up each morning, look yourself in the eye, and say your power phrase—make it a great day!

TACTICAL SUCCESS KEY:
It may seem silly at first, but this is your personal morning pep talk! You want to have a great day full of wonderful things? Then tell yourself that, and get ready to make it happen! It all begins in our minds—everything else will follow!

MY NEIGHBORHIVE MISSION DEBRIEFING
mission completion date ....

how do you feel after completing the sting operation?

....

....

....

what did you notice afterwards?
- about your mission target
- yourself/team
- surroundings/neighborhive

....

....

what will you want to do again with this mission to make your target feel special/that you made a difference?

....

....

....

what ideas do you have for your next sting ops mission?

....

....

....

OFFER A FREE NIGHT OF CHILDCARE TO A FRIEND OR NEIGHBOR HIVER AROUND THE HOLIDAY SEASON
solo op or team op

23

TARGET: Friends, family members, or fellow neighbor hivers

TIME: 03:00+

COST: $

MISSION OBJECTIVE:

Provide a free night of childcare to someone you know around the holiday season so he or she can use the time do some holiday prep.

GEAR & PROVISIONS:

- Dates and times you're available to help
- Age-appropriate activities to do with the children you're watching

☑ PREP STEP:

Be aware that single parents are especially in need of this sting-ops mission!

⏱ GO TIME!

1. Make yourself available, communicate the dates and times you could provide childcare, then schedule with your mission target.

2. Gather activities to do with the children you'll watch.

3. Have fun, and keep your focus on giving!

⚷ TACTICAL SUCCESS KEY:

Ask the parents in advance what type of activities their children like to do. Make sure they're safe, hydrated and fed, clean, and entertained. And then try to leave their place in a better state than when you found it (but don't go overboard).

MY NEIGHBORHIVE MISSION DEBRIEFING
mission completion date ....

how do you feel after completing the sting operation?

....

....

....

what did you notice afterwards?
- about your mission target
- yourself/team
- surroundings/neighborhive

....

what will you want to do again with this mission to make your target feel special/that
you made a difference?

....

....

....

what ideas do you have for your next sting ops mission?

....

....

....

HOLD THE DOOR OPEN FOR OTHERS

solo op

24

TARGET: Person approaching a doorway

TIME: 00:02

COST: $

MISSION OBJECTIVE:

Brighten someone's day by noticing him or her and being helpful—open a door and, if possible, help carry his or her gear.

GEAR & PROVISIONS:

- Open eyes to see the opportunity
- Sense of urgency to take action
- Smile and genuine heart to serve others

PREP STEP:

Be aware of your surroundings.

GO TIME!

1. Notice your target.

2. Smile!

3. Open door(s) and offer to help carry any bags, boxes, or other gear (but do so only if the person accepts, of course).

4. Wish him or her a pleasant day!

TACTICAL SUCCESS KEY:

Being aware of opportunities to be caring and helpful is key. Then take action! Spreading the sunshine through little acts of kindness makes a huge difference when we acknowledge and help others, especially when they least expect it.

MY NEIGHBORHIVE MISSION DEBRIEFING
mission completion date ....

how do you feel after completing the sting operation?

....

....

....

what did you notice afterwards?
- about your mission target
- yourself/team
- surroundings/neighborhive

....

....

what will you want to do again with this mission to make your target feel special/that you made a difference?

....

....

....

what ideas do you have for your next sting ops mission?

....

....

....

PREPARE A MEAL FOR A GRIEVING FAMILY

25

solo op or team op

TARGET: A grieving family in your neighborhive

TIME: 00:35+

COST: $-$$$

MISSION OBJECTIVE:

Bring some nourishment and sunshine to a grieving family by preparing and delivering a meal.

GEAR & PROVISIONS:

- Handwritten note
- Online resources for menu ideas, including options that freeze well
- A list of any food allergies or aversions or dietary restrictions you need to consider

PREP STEP:

Ask a friend of the family for dietary details if you aren't close to your target family.

GO TIME!

1. Find out the specific meal needs of the family (how many people, any allergies, etc.).

2. Decide on a meal idea, gather the ingredients, prepare the meal, and write a note to include.

3. Deliver the meal when the family is home. If they aren't, arrange for a friend of the family to deliver the meal when the time is right.

TACTICAL SUCCESS KEY:

Keep in mind that people who are grieving have things on their mind other than your act of kindness—so it's just fine if they don't acknowledge the meal! Sting-ops missions aren't about recognition; they're about care. It's also OK if they decline the meal. No matter the circumstances around your mission, send the target family positive energy and comforting thoughts in their time of sadness.

MY NEIGHBORHIVE MISSION DEBRIEFING
mission completion date

how do you feel after completing the sting operation?

what did you notice afterwards?
* about your mission target
* yourself/team
* surroundings/neighborhive

what will you want to do again with this mission to make your target feel special/that you made a difference?

what ideas do you have for your next sting ops mission?

EAT LOCAL, AND EAT ORGANIC WHENEVER POSSIBLE

26

solo op or team op

TARGET: You and your family
TIME: Varies, ongoing
COST: $-$$$

🎯 MISSION OBJECTIVE:
Eat well, *bee* well!

⚙️ GEAR & PROVISIONS:
- Participation in a community-supported agriculture (CSA) program
- In-season schedule of crops to plan your shopping
- Online resources about farmers' market locations and schedules
- Menu-planning ideas
- An interest in cultivating a friendship with your local farmer

☑️ PREP STEP:
Check out the farmers' markets in your community, and have fun trying new things from your neighborhive growers!

🕐 GO TIME!
1. Ask local organic farmers lots of questions about their growing practices.
2. Shop at farmers' markets and co-ops; join a CSA to maximize your dollars spent.
3. Find out where your grocery store's produce is sourced to make educated decisions on what you're feeding yourself and family.

🔑 TACTICAL SUCCESS KEY:
Purchase produce at local farmers' markets to support area growers and enjoy fresher food. Join a CSA program, co-op, and so on to stretch your dollars as you shop and eat for wellness!

MY NEIGHBORHIVE MISSION DEBRIEFING
mission completion date ....

how do you feel after completing the sting operation?

....

....

....

what did you notice afterwards?

- about your mission target
- yourself/team
- surroundings/neighborhive

....

....

....

what will you want to do again with this mission to make your target feel special/that you made a difference?

....

....

....

what ideas do you have for your next sting ops mission?

....

....

....

COLLECT COLD-WEATHER GEAR FOR THE HOMELESS IN YOUR COMMUNITY
team op

27

TARGET: Homeless people in your neighborhive

TIME: 01:30

COST: $-$$$

🎯 MISSION OBJECTIVE:

Bring warmth and sunshine to the homeless people in your community with coats, hats, gloves, boots, and other gear for cold or inclement weather!

⚙️ GEAR & PROVISIONS:

- Genuine, caring attitude
- Team of gear donors and collectors
- Bags or boxes
- Local organization to accept your donated items

☑️ PREP STEP:

Consider partnering with other local groups for this sting op—service groups to find and collect the gear and an organization that can distribute the cold-weather gear to needy folks in your area.

🕐 GO TIME!

1. Gather your team and connect to an organization that will accept the donated gear.

2. Collect new and gently used cold-weather gear.

3. Bring the items to the local organization that will distribute the donated items to those who need them.

📍 TACTICAL SUCCESS KEY:

By partnering with an organization that already serves the homeless and needy in your community, you can maximize your efforts and know you're making a big difference! Spread even more sunshine by including a handwritten note of encouragement to tuck into a jacket pocket or safety-pin to a hat, scarf, glove, and so on. You're awesome, neighborhive ninjas!

MY NEIGHBORHIVE MISSION DEBRIEFING
mission completion date
....

how do you feel after completing the sting operation?

....

....

what did you notice afterwards?
....
* about your mission target
* yourself/team   ....
* surroundings/neighborhive   ....

....

what will you want to do again with this mission to make your target feel special/that you made a difference?

....

....

what ideas do you have for your next sting ops mission?

....

....

LEARN SOMETHING BY LISTENING TO OTHERS FIRST BEFORE SPEAKING
solo op

28

TARGET: You and everyone around you

TIME: Ongoing

COST: $

MISSION OBJECTIVE:
Be open to learning new things by listening to others before speaking.

GEAR & PROVISIONS:
- Closed mouth
- Mindful active-listening skills
- A heart that puts others first
- Patience—you'll have your turn to speak

PREP STEP:
Make it your goal to be the best listener you know! You'll be giving yourself the gift of learning new things, and you'll be giving others the gift of respect. You get what you give!

GO TIME!
1. Pay attention and use your active-listening skills.
2. Restate or clarify what your target has said before responding.
3. Take your time before responding with clear thoughts spoken from the heart. (Keep your tone and body language in mind. Ask yourself: How is he or she receiving this from me?)

TACTICAL SUCCESS KEY:
There are many ways to communicate effectively, but troubles always seem to rise out of high emotion, misunderstanding, or feeling disrespected. By taking care to be an extra-great listener, we'll learn so much about those around us—and, in the process, give as valuable a gift to others as we do to ourselves.

MY NEIGHBORHIVE MISSION DEBRIEFING
mission completion date _____

how do you feel after completing the sting operation?

_____

_____

_____

what did you notice afterwards?
- about your mission target
- yourself/team
- surroundings/neighborhive

_____

_____

what will you want to do again with this mission to make your target feel special/that you made a difference?

_____

_____

_____

what ideas do you have for your next sting ops mission?

_____

_____

_____

READ TO KIDS

29

solo op or team op

TARGET: Kids!
TIME: 00:45+
COST: $

MISSION OBJECTIVE:
Reading books to kids!

GEAR & PROVISIONS:
- Local organization or hospital to partner with
- Appropriate books (if not provided)
- Friendly and fun mind-set
- Time set aside in advance

PREP STEP:
Contact local organizations in advance, since they may have a formal process to complete before you can help out. Practice reading books aloud in a fun way!

GO TIME!
1. Find a good place you can volunteer, and make contact with the appropriate person.
2. Set aside time and follow through.
3. Practice reading; read; have fun!

TACTICAL SUCCESS KEY:
Everyone loves a great story—bring it to life! This is a great opportunity to have fun and make connections with kids who are hungry for knowledge! You've got this!

MY NEIGHBORHIVE MISSION DEBRIEFING
mission completion date ....

how do you feel after completing the sting operation?

....

....

....

what did you notice afterwards?
- about your mission target
- yourself/team
- surroundings/neighborhive

....

....

....

what will you want to do again with this mission to make your target feel special/that you made a difference?

....

....

....

what ideas do you have for your next sting ops mission?

....

....

....

RECOGNIZE OTHERS' RANDOM ACTS OF KINDNESS AND ENCOURAGEMENT

solo op or team op

30

TARGET: Friends, family, coworkers, classmates, and your neighbor hivers

TIME: 00:05+

COST: $

⊚ MISSION OBJECTIVE:

Catch others doing good, and praise their efforts.

⚙ GEAR & PROVISIONS:

- Smile and authenticity
- Ninja vision to catch fellow sting operatives in acts of kindness or encouragement

☑ PREP STEP:

We want to make a difference, but we can't do it all on our own! Encouraging others to keep up the good work is just as important as doing good for others yourself!

⊙ GO TIME!

Be ready to offer up some kudos when you see someone doing good. For example:

"We need more people like you in the world! Thank you for your example!"

"Way to make a difference! You're awesome!"

"I could tell that what you said to that person really lifted her spirits!"

⚷ TACTICAL SUCCESS KEY:

Everyone can use encouragement, especially those out there who are pouring it out to others! Use your ninja vision to catch people in their acts of kindness, cheer them on, and be inspired when you notice another way to make a difference! See? Good things are happening all around you! You're an important part of spreading the sunshine worldwide!

MY NEIGHBORHIVE MISSION DEBRIEFING
mission completion date ....

how do you feel after completing the sting operation?

....
....
....

what did you notice afterwards?
- about your mission target
- yourself/team
- surroundings/neighborhive

....

what will you want to do again with this mission to make your target feel special/that
you made a difference?

....
....
....

what ideas do you have for your next sting ops mission?

....
....
....

MORE LIVING POTTED PLANTS AT HOME AND WORK, FEWER ARTIFICIAL AIR FRESHENERS

solo op or team op

31

TARGET: You, your family, your coworkers

TIME: 00:10+

COST: $-$$$

MISSION OBJECTIVE:

Fill your spaces with nature's air fresheners: living plants!

GEAR & PROVISIONS:

- Green potted plants
- Sunlight
- Water

PREP STEP:

Visit your local hardware store or home-and-garden center to learn about oxygenating plants for your *envirohive*!

GO TIME!

1. Purchase plants you love and that are suited to the environment they'll occupy.

2. Make sure they get sunlight and water.

3. Breathe in deeply!

TACTICAL SUCCESS KEY:

Chemical air fresheners just can't match the power of plants! Have fun tending your plants and watching them grow. And notice how much better it feels to breathe the indoor air all around you!

MY NEIGHBORHIVE MISSION DEBRIEFING
mission completion date ....

how do you feel after completing the sting operation?

....
....
....

what did you notice afterwards?
- about your mission target
- yourself/team
- surroundings/neighborhive

....
....
....

what will you want to do again with this mission to make your target feel special/that you made a difference?

....
....
....

what ideas do you have for your next sting ops mission?

....
....
....

PLAN A FAMILY GAME NIGHT

team op

32

TARGET: Your family and neighbor hivers

TIME: 01:00+

COST: $-$$

🎯 MISSION OBJECTIVE:

Enjoy some friendly competition at a family game night!

⚙️ GEAR & PROVISIONS:

- Scheduled time for a game night
- Beverages and snacks
- Games
- Fun music

☑️ PREP STEP:

Ask your family members what would make game night the most fun for them—incorporate everyone's ideas, and take turns selecting the games, music, and snacks.

🕐 GO TIME!

1. Schedule the game night.
2. Get ready with different games, music, and snacks!
3. Play your little ninja hearts out!

📍 TACTICAL SUCCESS KEY:

Have a blast playing games and connecting with family. Invite fellow neighbor hivers over and encourage them to have their own family game night. Maybe a tournament for all the neighborhive families is in order! Now that's winning!

MY NEIGHBORHIVE MISSION DEBRIEFING
mission completion date ....

how do you feel after completing the sting operation?

....

....

....

what did you notice afterwards?
- about your mission target
- yourself/team
- surroundings/neighborhive

....

....

what will you want to do again with this mission to make your target feel special/that you made a difference?

....

....

....

what ideas do you have for your next sting ops mission?

....

....

....

BE HELPFUL TO SOMEONE WHO IS MOVING

solo op or team op

33

TARGET: Fellow neighbor hivers
TIME: 02:00+
COST: $

🎯 MISSION OBJECTIVE:
Moving is never easy! Lighten your neighbor's load by sharing your time and skills.

⚙️ GEAR & PROVISIONS:
- "How can I best help?" mentality
- Boxes, packing tape, labels, or markers—if your neighbor hiver needs them
- If your neighbor hiver needs help carrying items, will a dolly or hand truck be available?
- Time frame to commit to and follow through on

☑️ PREP STEP:
Ask in advance how you can best help. This gives your neighbor the opportunity to think about and plan the moving activities to best utilize your help.

🕐 GO TIME!
1. Volunteer to help—share what you can do and for how long.
2. Plan it out, and commit to a specific date and time.
3. Help as much as you can, hydrate, and send your neighbor on a safe moving journey. Your sunshine will go with him or her to a new neighborhive!

🔑 TACTICAL SUCCESS KEY:
Everyone has a different approach to moving and time lines. Clarify in advance what the ideal situation will look like, what you're able to do, and what time you'll need to leave (if applicable). Remember proper lifting techniques, and be safe with those heavy boxes!

MY NEIGHBORHIVE MISSION DEBRIEFING
mission completion date ....

how do you feel after completing the sting operation?

....

....

what did you notice afterwards?
- about your mission target
- yourself/team
- surroundings/neighborhive

what will you want to do again with this mission to make your target feel special/that you made a difference?

....

....

what ideas do you have for your next sting ops mission?

....

....

DONATE TEACHING SUPPLIES TO A LOCAL CLASSROOM

34

solo op or team op

TARGET: The teacher and students of a local classroom

TIME: 00:35+

COST: $-$$$

MISSION OBJECTIVE:

Set your local educators up for success. Budding minds need care and resources—and teachers need our help with young hivers!

GEAR & PROVISIONS:

- Deserving classroom
- School supplies for teachers and students

PREP STEP:

Learn about the specific needs of a local teacher and classroom so you know what items to provide.

GO TIME!

1. Discover the supply needs of a specific classroom.

2. Shop and gather appropriate learning tools and resources.

3. Donate the supplies to a deserving classroom full of students eager to learn and grow!

TACTICAL SUCCESS KEY:

Though schools receive funding, many important classroom needs aren't covered by taxes—and teachers often cover the additional expenses themselves. Reach out to a class that could use your help. *Bee* on alert to other ways you can support learning in your community.

MY NEIGHBORHIVE MISSION DEBRIEFING
mission completion date ....

how do you feel after completing the sting operation?

....

....

....

what did you notice afterwards?
- about your mission target
- yourself/team
- surroundings/neighborhive

....

....

what will you want to do again with this mission to make your target feel special/that you made a difference?

....

....

....

what ideas do you have for your next sting ops mission?

....

....

....

CARPOOL

team op

TARGET: Coworkers, classmates, and neighbor hivers

TIME: 00:25+

COST: $

🎯 MISSION OBJECTIVE:

Share your ride to school or work to save resources; use the carpool lane; and connect with someone too!

⚙️ GEAR & PROVISIONS:

- Team attitude
- Shared ground rules
- Schedule agreed upon in advance
- Backup plan for when it doesn't work last minute

☑️ PREP STEP:

Check online directories to see if there's an established ride-share organization you can plug into if you don't know anyone to carpool with when you begin.

🕐 GO TIME!

1. Find a carpool buddy or group.
2. Communicate shared expectations, ground rules, and schedule.
3. Follow your plan, and enjoy the ride!

🔑 TACTICAL SUCCESS KEY:

Communication is the key to respecting each other's time, schedules, and vehicles. Talk about your plan of action if someone is running late or weather conditions are poor. Strategize about who will drive when, how to handle vacation time, and so on. Discussing potential complications in advance will make the experience more enjoyable as you help each other save resources and time. Safe travels!

MY NEIGHBORHIVE MISSION DEBRIEFING
mission completion date ....

how do you feel after completing the sting operation?

....

....

what did you notice afterwards?
- about your mission target
- yourself/team
- surroundings/neighborhive

....

....

what will you want to do again with this mission to make your target feel special/that you made a difference?

....

....

what ideas do you have for your next sting ops mission?

....

....

BRAINSTORM WAYS TO MAKE A DIFFERENCE WITH LOCAL STUDENTS
team op

36

TARGET: Your community
TIME: Ongoing
COST: $

🎯 MISSION OBJECTIVE:
Get MAD-storming with your local students in mind. (That's make-a-difference brainstorming!)

⚙️ GEAR & PROVISIONS:
- The listening skills of a ninja
- Notepad and writing utensil

☑️ PREP STEP:
Ask local students what they would like to see change for the better in the community, and encourage them to share their ideas about how to create those improvements.

🕐 GO TIME!
1. Connect with students.
2. Ask inspiring and clarifying questions.
3. Take careful notes, and listen well.
4. Help them champion change, and be their raving fan!

📍 TACTICAL SUCCESS KEY:
Brainstorm different ways to implement positive change. Ask questions that prompt the students to elaborate on their ideas. Remind the group that everyone has something valuable to contribute—and when we all work together, massive progress will be made! *Boom!*

MY NEIGHBORHIVE MISSION DEBRIEFING
mission completion date ....

how do you feel after completing the sting operation?

....
....
....

what did you notice afterwards?
- about your mission target
- yourself/team
- surroundings/neighborhive

....
....
....

what will you want to do again with this mission to make your target feel special/that you made a difference?

....
....
....

what ideas do you have for your next sting ops mission?

....
....
....

CLEAN AND DECLUTTER YOUR HOUSE, AND THEN DONATE WHAT YOU AREN'T USING ANYMORE

solo op or team op

37

TARGET: You and your home
TIME: 01:30+
COST: $-$$$

🎯 MISSION OBJECTIVE:

Beeline to streamline! Clean and declutter your house and then donate the things you're no longer using.

⚙️ GEAR & PROVISIONS:

- Can-do, don't-need-it attitude!
- Garbage bags & cleaning supplies
- Boxes and other organizational tools
- Organization where you can donate unnecessary but usable belongings

☑️ PREP STEP:

Get excited about getting rid of items you don't love or use regularly—and if there are other hivers in your home, work together to make this a fun activity as you go!

🕐 GO TIME!

1. Make three piles: toss, give away, and keep.

2. Go through one room at a time. Take a break if you start to feel overwhelmed.

3. Make progress, take out the trash, donate the usable items, organize, and then feel great about how you've improved your hive!

🔑 TACTICAL SUCCESS KEY:

Be aware of how you're feeling during the process. If it starts to become a negative experience, it's important to get some support or step away for a bit. This is hard work, but it should feel good to get rid of anything that's mucking up your hive. You've got this!

MY NEIGHBORHIVE MISSION DEBRIEFING
mission completion date

how do you feel after completing the sting operation?

what did you notice afterwards?
- about your mission target
- yourself/team
- surroundings/neighborhive

what will you want to do again with this mission to make your target feel special/that you made a difference?

what ideas do you have for your next sting ops mission?

PICK UP TRASH

team op

38

TARGET: Your neighborhive
TIME: 00:05+
COST: $

 MISSION OBJECTIVE:

Beautify (or rather, *beeautify*) your neighborhive by leaving it in a better state than you found it!

GEAR & PROVISIONS:

- Ninja vision to see the opportunities to help!
- Trash bags and gloves

PREP STEP:

Bee safe as you pick up discarded items—let others know where you'll be, and protect your hands from germs and sharp items by wearing gloves.

GO TIME!

1. Pick up trash while out and about in your community.
2. Dispose of trash in the proper receptacles or designated areas.
3. Wash your hands and keep your ninja vision ready for the next opportunity!

TACTICAL SUCCESS KEY:

Practice cleaning up as you go in and out of your home for a great habit to model for others. You're rocking this, ninja! *Yes!*

MY NEIGHBORHIVE MISSION DEBRIEFING
mission completion date ....

how do you feel after completing the sting operation?

....

....

....

what did you notice afterwards?
- about your mission target ....
- yourself/team ....
- surroundings/neighborhive ....

....

what will you want to do again with this mission to make your target feel special/that you made a difference?

....

....

....

what ideas do you have for your next sting ops mission?

....

....

....

"ADOPT" A GRANDPARENT

solo op or team op

39

TARGET: Elderly neighbor hivers
TIME: 01:30+
COST: $

🎯 MISSION OBJECTIVE:

Make a connection with an elderly neighbor hiver to share the love and sunshine!

⚙️ GEAR & PROVISIONS:

- Respect, caring, and kindness
- Partnership with a local organization

☑️ PREP STEP:

Give love, care, and kindness to someone who may be lonely, and learn something from him or her at the same time!

🕐 GO TIME!

1. Partner with a local organization to find a grandparent to "adopt."

2. Commit time to spend and then follow through.

3. Enjoy the gift of friendship, caring, and fun as you spend time with this incredible individual!

🔑 TACTICAL SUCCESS KEY:

Completing this sting-ops mission is likely to show you that you're receiving more than you're giving! That's the best feeling in the world! Keep in mind that it may take some time to break the ice and get to know one another, but it's well worth your patience and care!

MY NEIGHBORHIVE MISSION DEBRIEFING
mission completion date ....

how do you feel after completing the sting operation?

....

....

....

what did you notice afterwards?
- about your mission target   ....
- yourself/team   ....
- surroundings/neighborhive   ....

....

what will you want to do again with this mission to make your target feel special/that you made a difference?

....

....

....

what ideas do you have for your next sting ops mission?

....

....

....

WASH SOMEONE'S CAR ON A SUNNY DAY

solo op or team op

TARGET: Friend, family member, or neighbor hiver

TIME: 00:25+

COST: $

⌖ MISSION OBJECTIVE:

Let yourself soak up the sun as you spread sunshine by washing someone's car on a warm day.

⚙ GEAR & PROVISIONS:

- Attention to detail
- Respectful behavior
- Cleaning products and tools approved by the vehicle's owner
- Water source
- Sunshine for quick and even drying

☑ PREP STEP:

Be sure to ask the vehicle's owner for permission before doing this mission.

Also confirm which cleaning products he or she approves.

🕒 GO TIME!

1. Seek approval from the vehicle's owner before beginning your sting-ops mission.

2. Arrange a time and place for washing the vehicle in advance.

3. Obtain owner-approved cleaning products and tools.

4. Wash it, rinse it, dry it—and enjoy being outdoors!

⚲ TACTICAL SUCCESS KEY:

Keep in mind that some friends, family members, and neighbor hivers may not wish to accept this specific act of kindness. That's OK! This mission is about spreading the sunshine, so even if they decline, wish them a great day and you do the same!

MY NEIGHBORHIVE MISSION DEBRIEFING
mission completion date ....

how do you feel after completing the sting operation?

....

....

....

what did you notice afterwards?
- about your mission target
- yourself/team
- surroundings/neighborhive

....

....

what will you want to do again with this mission to make your target feel special/that
you made a difference?

....

....

....

what ideas do you have for your next sting ops mission?

....

....

....

TARGET: You

TIME: 00:20+ per day

COST: $-$$$

MISSION OBJECTIVE:

Take time for yourself each day to learn something new, develop a skill, and work toward achieving your next life goal!

GEAR & PROVISIONS:

- Journal
- Clear idea of your goals!
- A vision board for pictures of your dreams
- Books, audiobooks, online resources, seminars, and workshops
- Coach or mentor—maybe both!

PREP STEP:

Have some fun dreaming up your goals so you can work toward living them!

Remember that life isn't about "someday when"—take joy in the journey too!

GO TIME!

1. Start with one or two things to think about or work on for just a few minutes a day.

2. Create lists of your short- and long-term goals—and have fun with it!

3. Set aside consistent time for yourself each day (whether it's twenty minutes or an hour). This is a gift to your current and future selves. It's not a chore. :-)

4. Reflect on what's working and what isn't; make adjustments to your approach.

TACTICAL SUCCESS KEY:

Remember that personal development takes time and practice, so *bee* kind to yourself when it seems like your goal is far off. Just keep growing and keep going!

MY NEIGHBORHIVE MISSION DEBRIEFING
mission completion date ....

how do you feel after completing the sting operation?

....

....

....

what did you notice afterwards?
- about your mission target
- yourself/team
- surroundings/neighborhive

....

....

what will you want to do again with this mission to make your target feel special/that
you made a difference?

....

....

....

what ideas do you have for your next sting ops mission?

....

....

....

CONSERVE WATER AND ENERGY AT HOME AND AT THE OFFICE

42

solo op or team op

TARGET: Home and office

TIME: 00:15+

COST: $

🎯 MISSION OBJECTIVE:

Save it! Take steps to conserve water and energy at your home and office.

⚙️ GEAR & PROVISIONS:

- Ninja vision to notice where waste is happening
- Lightning-fast reflexes to flip the light switches when going in and out of rooms

☑️ PREP STEP:

Having an awareness of how resources are being used will help you brainstorm ideas to conserve water and energy. You'll start to see opportunities all around you. Work together, ninjas!

🕐 GO TIME!

1. Spark a conversation about using resources wisely at home and work.

2. Collaborate with your fellow worker bees and hivemates to conserve energy and minimize waste.

🔑 TACTICAL SUCCESS KEY:

Resources are important both in and out of our hives. By being mindful of our usage and minimizing waste, we can optimize our resources and support a healthier neighborhive and world!

MY NEIGHBORHIVE MISSION DEBRIEFING
mission completion date
....

how do you feel after completing the sting operation?

....
....
....

what did you notice afterwards?
- about your mission target
- yourself/team
- surroundings/neighborhive

....
....
....

what will you want to do again with this mission to make your target feel special/that you made a difference?

....
....
....

what ideas do you have for your next sting ops mission?

....
....
....

TEACH A COMMUNITY-EDUCATION CLASS

solo op or team op

43

TARGET: Your neighbor hivers!

TIME: 01:00+

COST: $

MISSION OBJECTIVE:

Share your knowledge and experience by leading a community-education class.

GEAR & PROVISIONS:

- Content or topic to teach
- Visual aids and class activities
- Course outline and step-by-step plan

PREP STEP:

We all have special skills and unique value to add to the world. Think about what useful or fun skills you can teach others. Get inspired by reading descriptions of current or past community-ed courses.

GO TIME!

1. Brainstorm ideas for your course's topic.

2. Partner with a local organization related to your subject to get started.

3. Create a course outline and gather class materials.

4. Rehearse delivery of the class to increase your comfort level.

5. Have fun, smile often, be patient with yourself and others—and rock it, neighborhive ninja!

TACTICAL SUCCESS KEY:

Think about the good things you're known for, what you enjoy doing, and how you could help others enjoy it as much as you do. Remember that there are many learning styles and approaches to training, so keep your focus on helping others and having patience as you go through the process together. Keep growing and going!

MY NEIGHBORHIVE MISSION DEBRIEFING
mission completion date ....

how do you feel after completing the sting operation?

....

....

....

what did you notice afterwards?
- about your mission target
- yourself/team
- surroundings/neighborhive

....

....

....

what will you want to do again with this mission to make your target feel special/that you made a difference?

....

....

....

what ideas do you have for your next sting ops mission?

....

....

....

INVITE A NEIGHBOR HIVER OVER FOR DINNER

solo op or team op

44

TARGET: Neighbor hiver(s)

TIME: Varies

COST: $-$$$

MISSION OBJECTIVE:

Invite a neighbor to come over for dinner. Let the sunshine in!

GEAR & PROVISIONS:

- Friendly attitude
- A few options for date and time
- Menu ideas (keep it simple)
- Ingredients
- Flexibility and grace

PREP STEP:

Be proactively mindful and considerate of any dietary restrictions, food aversions, or allergies by asking your guest(s) in advance as a courtesy.

GO TIME!

1. Invite neighbor hiver(s) over for dinner.
2. Prepare a meal to share.
3. Spend time getting to know your neighbor hiver(s) over dinner—and have fun!

TACTICAL SUCCESS KEY:

Bee yourself, and know that not everyone will accept your invitation—that's OK! If for some reason what you prepare doesn't turn out, or your guest is unable to partake, do your best to not take it personally. The most important thing is to share kindness, connect with your fellow neighbor hiver, and have a great time (even if you burn the meatloaf and have to order takeout). Relax. Everybody eats, so keep it simple and fun!

MY NEIGHBORHIVE MISSION DEBRIEFING
mission completion date ....

how do you feel after completing the sting operation?

....

....

what did you notice afterwards?   ....
- about your mission target
- yourself/team   ....
- surroundings/neighborhive   ....

....

what will you want to do again with this mission to make your target feel special/that you made a difference?

....

....

what ideas do you have for your next sting ops mission?

....

....

....

MAKE A WALL OF SUNSHINE TO CELEBRATE ACTS OF KINDNESS AND ENCOURAGEMENT

solo op or team op

45

TARGET: Your home, classroom, or workplace

TIME: 00:15+

COST: $-$$

MISSION OBJECTIVE:

Create places to mark and celebrate everyday actions that are kind and encouraging to others.

GEAR & PROVISIONS:

- Wall space
- Note cards, sticky notes, and the like to record all the kindness
- Ninja vision to catch others doing acts of kindness and encouragement!

PREP STEP:

Get ready to bumble!!! Set up your board as a team and talk about how it works so you can all participate!

GO TIME!

1. Set up your wall of sunshine in a common area that's easily accessed!

2. Keep sticky notes and markers close by. Or use note cards along with ways to post them on the wall (e.g., tape or pushpins).

3. Catch people in their acts of kindness and encouragement, post them, and celebrate!

TACTICAL SUCCESS KEY:

The wall of sunshine is only for acknowledging acts of kindness and encouragement—not chores at home, grades or extra credit at school, or performance-based achievements at work. Call people out by name and describe what they did to make a difference, big or small, and then celebrate in fun, creative ways!

MY NEIGHBORHIVE MISSION DEBRIEFING
mission completion date
....

how do you feel after completing the sting operation?

....

....

....

what did you notice afterwards?
- about your mission target
- yourself/team
- surroundings/neighborhive

....

....

....

....

what will you want to do again with this mission to make your target feel special/that you made a difference?

....

....

....

what ideas do you have for your next sting ops mission?

....

....

....

BE CURIOUS, ASK QUESTIONS, AND SEEK TO UNDERSTAND MORE IN CONVERSATIONS
solo op

46

TARGET: Family, friends, and neighbor hivers

TIME: Daily

COST: $

🎯 MISSION OBJECTIVE:

Better conversations! Your curiosity and careful listening will pay off. Better communities begin with better conversations!

⚙️ GEAR & PROVISIONS:

- A focus on others
- Willingness to learn
- Two-eared (and closed-mouth) approach to listening
- Care, kindness, courtesy

☑️ PREP STEP:

Good communication is the cornerstone of great relationships—and good relationships help change the world for the better! Remember, change begins with you.

🕐 GO TIME!

1. Don't just hear—*listen*.
2. Wait . . . and a wait little more . . . .
3. Ask clarifying questions before making assumptions about the speaker's intent.
4. Wait . . . and then restate what the person said to make sure you fully understood him or her.
5. Listen, wait, and respond thoughtfully—taking care with each step.

🔑 TACTICAL SUCCESS KEY:

Keep in mind that good communication skills take time to grow. Do your best, be patient, and ask yourself what you learned with each new experience. Start by aiming to be the best listener you can be, and build from there. We all want to be heard and understood; give that to others, and it will be given to you. We get what we give!

MY NEIGHBORHIVE MISSION DEBRIEFING
mission completion date ....

how do you feel after completing the sting operation?

....

....

what did you notice afterwards?
- about your mission target
- yourself/team
- surroundings/neighborhive

....

....

....

what will you want to do again with this mission to make your target feel special/that you made a difference?

....

....

....

what ideas do you have for your next sting ops mission?

....

....

....

ORGANIZE A COMMUNITY CLEANUP DAY WITH YOUR NEIGHBORS
team op

47

TARGET: Your neighborhive
TIME: 03:00+
COST: $-$$$

MISSION OBJECTIVE:

Initiate and arrange a community cleanup day with your neighbor hivers.

GEAR & PROVISIONS:

- Service and add-value mentality
- Trash bags and gloves
- Areas of focus and duties within those areas

PREP STEP:

Check with city administration to see if there are guidelines to follow while helping to clean up the community (specific parking areas, wearing safety vests, waste handling and disposal, etc.).

GO TIME!

1. Get your sting-ops team ready to rock!
2. Pick up trash in your community.
3. Responsibly dispose of the collected trash.
4. Clean yourself up, and then celebrate a job well done with your team!

TACTICAL SUCCESS KEY:

Whether you spend a half hour or an entire day cleaning up your community, every little bit counts! Look for opportunities to keep your neighborhive happy and healthy. Make it fun!

MY NEIGHBORHIVE MISSION DEBRIEFING
mission completion date ....

how do you feel after completing the sting operation?

....

....

....

what did you notice afterwards?
- about your mission target   ....
- yourself/team   ....
- surroundings/neighborhive   ....

....

what will you want to do again with this mission to make your target feel special/that you made a difference?

....

....

....

what ideas do you have for your next sting ops mission?

....

....

....

ANONYMOUSLY SURPRISE A HARDWORKING COUPLE WITH A GIFT CARD FOR A DATE NIGHT
solo op or team op

48

TARGET: Hardworking couple in your neighborhive

TIME: 00:15+

COST: $–$$$

🎯 MISSION OBJECTIVE:

Date-night surprise!

⚙️ GEAR & PROVISIONS:

- Gift card to cover their date-night expenses
- Ninja vision and stealth skills to leave the gift card for them to find

☑️ PREP STEP:

Do some behind-the-scenes investigating to find out where the couple likes to go on a date.

🕐 GO TIME!

1. Purchase gift card.
2. Leave the gift card for them to find (marked with "Date night!" or a similar short message).
3. Keep the op hush-hush!

🔑 TACTICAL SUCCESS KEY:

Keep it simple! You don't need to be extravagant—any amount on the gift card can be a great prompt for your hardworking targets to take a break and enjoy each other's company.

MY NEIGHBORHIVE MISSION DEBRIEFING
mission completion date
_____

how do you feel after completing the sting operation?

....

....

....

what did you notice afterwards?
- about your mission target
- yourself/team
- surroundings/neighborhive

....

....

....

....

what will you want to do again with this mission to make your target feel special/that you made a difference?

....

....

....

what ideas do you have for your next sting ops mission?

....

....

....

PACK MORE NUTRITIOUS LUNCHES

solo op or team op

49

TARGET: You (and your honeys at home)

TIME: 00:15

COST: $-$$

MISSION OBJECTIVE:

Treat yourself with care by preparing nutritious lunches to fuel happy, productive, healthy days!

GEAR & PROVISIONS:

- Reusable food packaging (e.g., portable containers)
- Coupons and weekly sales ads
- Meal-plan calendar
- Grocery list
- Online resources for healthy meal ideas

☑ PREP STEP:
Brainstorm healthy, balanced meal ideas and examine why healthy eating is important to you.

🕒 GO TIME!

1. Plan your week of meals and prepare your grocery list.
2. Go grocery shopping with money-saving resources.
3. Make the next day's lunch the night before to save time and keep you on track to follow your plan.

🔑 TACTICAL SUCCESS KEY:

Make a plan and do your grocery shopping after you've eaten a meal or snack. You'll be less likely to overspend and purchase unhealthy or unnecessary items. This sting-ops mission is even better when you team up with a friend or family member!

MY NEIGHBORHIVE MISSION DEBRIEFING
mission completion date

how do you feel after completing the sting operation?

what did you notice afterwards?
* about your mission target
* yourself/team
* surroundings/neighborhive

what will you want to do again with this mission to make your target feel special/that you made a difference?

what ideas do you have for your next sting ops mission?

GROW BEE-FRIENDLY PLANTS AND FLOWERS IN YOUR YARD

50

solo op or team op

TARGET: Bees and other pollinators
TIME: 01:30+
COST: $-$$$

🎯 MISSION OBJECTIVE:

Grow a bee buffet! Cultivating bee-friendly plants helps feed bees and other pollinators so they can continue to help feed the world!

⚙️ GEAR & PROVISIONS:

- Sunlight-exposed area for plants and flowers
- Plant-ready soil
- Seeds and plants that are friendly to area pollinators
- Online resources for planning and plant care
- Time to consistently feed, water, and weed

☑️ PREP STEP:

Research what plants and flowers your local pollinators can eat, and then focus on planting and caring for those.

🕐 GO TIME!

1. Research your local bees and pollinators. What can they eat?

2. Plan and plant your garden.

3. Water, feed, and weed your plants regularly.

4. Watch your bee buffet flourish!

🔑 TACTICAL SUCCESS KEY:

After you finish planning and planting your garden, be sure to give your bee-friendly plants consistent care. If bees visit you as you're tending to their bee buffet, please be gentle and don't swat them away. Bees sting if they feel threatened or alarmed, so either calmly keep caring for your garden, or come back to it at another time.

MY NEIGHBORHIVE MISSION DEBRIEFING
mission completion date ....

how do you feel after completing the sting operation?

....

....

....

what did you notice afterwards?
- about your mission target
- yourself/team
- surroundings/neighborhive

....

....

what will you want to do again with this mission to make your target feel special/that you made a difference?

....

....

....

what ideas do you have for your next sting ops mission?

....

....

....

CALL YOUR GRANDPARENT, AUNT, UNCLE, OR PARENT TO SHARE A MEMORY AND CATCH UP
solo op or team op

51

TARGET: Your family
TIME: 00:10+
COST: $

🎯 MISSION OBJECTIVE:
Stay connected to your family by staying in touch and remembering shared experiences.

⚙️ GEAR & PROVISIONS:

- Smile in your voice!
- Contact information
- Phone
- Just a few minutes of your time!

☑️ PREP STEP:
Your family members will love to hear from you! It's not a chore—it's a gift!

🕐 GO TIME!
Grab a free moment on the go or set aside time in advance, if that works better for you. Checking in with a "Hey, I've been thinking about you" sends a lot of long-distance sunshine to family members who get busy too, and miss you just the same!

🔑 TACTICAL SUCCESS KEY:
People like to feel special and remembered—especially your family! Even if you aren't able to talk for long, taking the initiative to dial and speak (not e-mail or text!) sends the real message: You care, and they matter!

MY NEIGHBORHIVE MISSION DEBRIEFING
mission completion date

how do you feel after completing the sting operation?

what did you notice afterwards?
- about your mission target
- yourself/team
- surroundings/neighborhive

what will you want to do again with this mission to make your target feel special/that you made a difference?

what ideas do you have for your next sting ops mission?

SHARE BOOKS AND MAGAZINES IN YOUR NEIGHBORHIVE

solo op or team op

52

TARGET: You and fellow neighbor hivers

TIME: Varies

COST: $-$$$

MISSION OBJECTIVE:

Create new opportunities to pass around great reading materials by building your own neighborhive library.

GEAR & PROVISIONS:

- Books and magazines
- Book box or another accessible and dry place to keep the reading materials

PREP STEP:

Check with city administration to see if there are any regulations about posted items outside of your home. After all, ninjas change the world, but they also follow local regulations and laws!

GO TIME!

1. Check your local regulations.
2. Gather books and magazines to share in your neighborhive.
3. Share, read, enjoy, repeat!

TACTICAL SUCCESS KEY:

You can tackle this sting-ops mission solo, but we highly recommend making it a team effort. Ask other neighbor hivers if they wish to contribute old books and magazines to the cause, and keep your hive full of great sharable resources! Yeah, ninja—you're keeping it sweet!

MY NEIGHBORHIVE MISSION DEBRIEFING
mission completion date ....

how do you feel after completing the sting operation?

....

....

....

what did you notice afterwards?
- about your mission target
- yourself/team
- surroundings/neighborhive

....

....

what will you want to do again with this mission to make your target feel special/that you made a difference?

....

....

....

what ideas do you have for your next sting ops mission?

....

....

....

FORGIVE OFTEN

solo op

53

TARGET: You and others
TIME: Ongoing
COST: $

🎯 MISSION OBJECTIVE:

Learn to forgive yourself, then forgive others. Repeat often.

⚙️ GEAR & PROVISIONS:

- Open mind and heart
- Grace for yourself and others
- Mindfulness moving forward with thoughts, words, and actions

☑️ PREP STEP:

Remember: Everyone is human, and we all make mistakes. We're in control of our own life and what kind of energy we put out into the world. When we hold on to pain, we block out good things that are waiting to come into our lives. Today is another opportunity to begin again!

🕐 GO TIME!

1. Consider the root of what's causing your pain and others' pain.

2. Think about what you *can* change, and acknowledge what you cannot.

3. Release the pain you hold or have caused to the universe, and be grateful for the lesson.

4. Focus on good thoughts, being careful with your words and actions, and staying kind to yourself and others as you move forward.

🔑 TACTICAL SUCCESS KEY:

The past can't be changed, but we can change our approach to how we treat ourselves and others starting *now*. We're all in this life together. Let's support and encourage one another as we keep going!

MY NEIGHBORHIVE MISSION DEBRIEFING
mission completion date ....

how do you feel after completing the sting operation?
....
....
....

what did you notice afterwards?
- about your mission target
- yourself/team
- surroundings/neighborhive

....

what will you want to do again with this mission to make your target feel special/that you made a difference?
....
....
....

what ideas do you have for your next sting ops mission?
....
....
....

SPARK AN ONGOING CONVERSATION ABOUT OPPORTUNITIES TO IMPROVE YOUR NEIGHBORHIVE
solo op or team op

54

TARGET: Your neighborhive
TIME: Varies, ongoing
COST: $

MISSION OBJECTIVE:
Encourage and cultivate a happy, healthy community!

GEAR & PROVISIONS:
- Openness to everyone's ideas
- Connection with fellow neighbor hivers

PREP STEP:
We all want to live in a happy, healthy community. Let everyone's ideas be heard, and become a catalyst for positive change by being a champion of others' thoughts and goals.

GO TIME!
1. Connect with your neighbor hivers. Don't be shy!

2. Start a conversation by asking great questions.

3. Encourage others to express their ideas, and help to champion those that foster positive change.

TACTICAL SUCCESS KEY:
This is a community-building activity, not an idea war! Listen to and support others, and they'll do the same for you! Everyone can change the world right from his or her own neighborhive, but it takes working together as a team. Remember that it's not a competition— we all share similar goals to live in a better place! We're in this together!

MY NEIGHBORHIVE MISSION DEBRIEFING
mission completion date ....

how do you feel after completing the sting operation?

....

....

....

what did you notice afterwards?
- about your mission target
- yourself/team
- surroundings/neighborhive

....

....

what will you want to do again with this mission to make your target feel special/that you made a difference?

....

....

....

what ideas do you have for your next sting ops mission?

....

....

....

HELP PREPARE A YOUNG PERSON FOR A CAREER BY HELPING HIM OR HER CRAFT A RÉSUMÉ

solo op or team op

55

TARGET: Young person in your community

TIME: Varies

COST: $

MISSION OBJECTIVE:

Support the career aspirations of young person for his or her chosen career by helping with a résumé.

GEAR & PROVISIONS:

- Online résumé-building resources
- Time blocked out to help
- Local organization to partner with

PREP STEP:

Get in touch with a local organization to express your volunteer interest in career-preparation programs. Perhaps you should consider focusing on a particular industry or job type.

GO TIME!

1. Connect with community organizations.

2. Set aside time for volunteering.

3. Follow through with your time commitment and focus on the young person you're helping. What are his or her goals? How can you help him or her prepare to pursue those goals?

TACTICAL SUCCESS KEY:

Decide in advance how much time you're willing to devote to this type of volunteering and if you wish to focus on career prep in a specific field or industry. Some programs will pair you with the same person for an extended time, while others change it up each time you volunteer. Ask good questions when doing your research with the organizations, and keep an open mind to opportunities you're not expecting.

MY NEIGHBORHIVE MISSION DEBRIEFING
mission completion date ....

how do you feel after completing the sting operation?

....
....
....

what did you notice afterwards?
- about your mission target
- yourself/team
- surroundings/neighborhive

....
....
....

what will you want to do again with this mission to make your target feel special/that you made a difference?

....
....
....

what ideas do you have for your next sting ops mission?

....
....
....

COMPLIMENT A CHILD ON HIS OR HER UNIQUE CONTRIBUTION TO THE WORLD
solo op

56

TARGET: A neighborhive child you know

TIME: 00:05

COST: $

MISSION OBJECTIVE:
Give a child a confidence boost by telling him or her that you notice the good he or she shares with others.

GEAR & PROVISIONS:
- Smile!
- Ninja vision to see a child's unique and amazing contribution to the world!

PREP STEP:
Remember that children are constantly learning and growing, so your words are very memorable and meaningful in their development!

GO TIME!
1. Catch a child in an act of kindness, giving great effort and showing heart, being a good friend to someone, showing honesty or caring, and so on.

2. Tell the child how great it is that he or she did that and to keep up the good work!

3. High fives and fist bumps are good too! Remember to thank the child for who he or she is and all the good he or she is doing!

TACTICAL SUCCESS KEY:
Children offer the world an incredible sense of wonder and a unique perspective we can miss in the bustle of life as an adult; they often see things we don't. Be genuine and uplifting, and cheer them on to greatness. They're wonderful people who bring so much to the world!

MY NEIGHBORHIVE MISSION DEBRIEFING
mission completion date ....

how do you feel after completing the sting operation?

....

....

....

what did you notice afterwards?
- about your mission target
- yourself/team
- surroundings/neighborhive

what will you want to do again with this mission to make your target feel special/that you made a difference?

....

....

....

what ideas do you have for your next sting ops mission?

....

....

....

FEED THE BIRDS

57

solo op or team op

TARGET: Community birds
TIME: 00:10+
COST: $-$$

MISSION OBJECTIVE:

Nourish your feathered neighborhive friends to bring sweetness to birds and bees!

GEAR & PROVISIONS:

- Knowledge of the types of birds that live in your community and what they can eat
- Appropriate bird food
- Bird feeder(s)

PREP STEP:

Discover and research which birds live in your community.

GO TIME!

1. Buy bird food.
2. Set up bird feeders in appropriate areas.
3. Feed the birds, and enjoy the view!

TACTICAL SUCCESS KEY:

Visit the library or research your local birds online. You're feeding the winged, but this is a beautiful viewing and learning experience for you! Be sure to select food that's safe for the birds to consume, and you may see your friends return for many seasons to come!

MY NEIGHBORHIVE MISSION DEBRIEFING
mission completion date

how do you feel after completing the sting operation?

what did you notice afterwards?
- about your mission target
- yourself/team
- surroundings/neighborhive

what will you want to do again with this mission to make your target feel special/that you made a difference?

what ideas do you have for your next sting ops mission?

VOLUNTEER MORE

solo op or team op

58

TARGET: Your chosen cause
TIME: Varies
COST: $

🎯 MISSION OBJECTIVE:

Volunteer more to directly impact your community in a positive way!

⚙️ GEAR & PROVISIONS:

- Online directory or resources and research time to find a cause you wish to support with your time and energy

- Time blocked out to volunteer

☑️ PREP STEP:

Research local causes and organizations where you can help make a difference from your own neighborhive!

🕐 GO TIME!

1. Research and select a cause.

2. Connect with a local chapter of the organization.

3. Commit time to volunteer and then follow through.

4. Keep up the great work making a difference!

📍 TACTICAL SUCCESS KEY:

Before you dive in fully to one organization, it's OK to "try on" a few to find the one that best fits your interests, your contribution style, and your schedule. Make some notes after each experience to gauge differences—and who knows, you may end up loving them all or picking a couple of different causes to share your volunteering time and energy. It's all jive in the neighborhive—so don't sweat it. Do new things and keep giving!

MY NEIGHBORHIVE MISSION DEBRIEFING
mission completion date

how do you feel after completing the sting operation?

....
....
....

what did you notice afterwards?
- about your mission target
- yourself/team
- surroundings/neighborhive

....
....
....

what will you want to do again with this mission to make your target feel special/that you made a difference?

....
....
....

what ideas do you have for your next sting ops mission?

....
....
....

HELP SOMEONE GET HOME WHO CAN'T ON HIS OR HER OWN

solo op or team op

59

TARGET: Stranded neighbor hiver
TIME: 00:15+
COST: $-$$$

MISSION OBJECTIVE:
Be a transportation problem solver.

GEAR & PROVISIONS:
- Care and concern for safety—yours and your stranded neighbor hiver's
- Taxi company and public transportation phone numbers
- Taxi or bus fare if you aren't driving your target home yourself

PREP STEP:
Personal safety is the most important part of this sting op!

GO TIME!
1. Ask your neighbor hiver if he or she has a ride home.
2. If not (and if you feel comfortable driving him or her home) offer a ride; alternately, call a taxi and provide the fare or look up the bus schedule and provide pass money.

TACTICAL SUCCESS KEY:
Ask your stranded neighbor hiver questions. If he or she is in an unsafe position to get home, try to assist. Remember to keep your own personal safety a priority when you help others.

MY NEIGHBORHIVE MISSION DEBRIEFING
mission completion date
....

how do you feel after completing the sting operation?

....

....

what did you notice afterwards?

- about your mission target
- yourself/team
- surroundings/neighborhive

....

....

....

....

what will you want to do again with this mission to make your target feel special/that you made a difference?

....

....

....

what ideas do you have for your next sting ops mission?

....

....

....

TREAT YOUR MAIL CARRIER

60

solo op or team op

TARGET: Neighborhive mail carrier
TIME: 00:05
COST: $

🎯 MISSION OBJECTIVE:

Treat your mail carrier! Leave your daily visitor a token of your appreciation in the form of a note and a gift card for a small indulgence (e.g., a local ice-cream shop or coffee shop).

⚙️ GEAR & PROVISIONS:

- Friendly note
- Gift card for a special treat

☑️ PREP STEP:

Be sure to label your note prominently so the mail carrier knows it's meant for him or her!

🕐 GO TIME!

1. Purchase a gift card.

2. Have your note and gift card ready and waiting before your usual mail-delivery time.

📍 TACTICAL SUCCESS KEY:

Keep in mind that neighborhive mail carriers are on the job and have a lot of ground to cover in their day's work (so they don't always have much time to chat). If your mail carrier is not able to accept your act of kindness—no worries! This is about spreading the sunshine, so even if it doesn't work out the way you planned, he or she will appreciate your thoughtfulness in wishing him or her a great day.

MY NEIGHBORHIVE MISSION DEBRIEFING
mission completion date ....

how do you feel after completing the sting operation?

....
....

what did you notice afterwards?   ....
- about your mission target   ....
- yourself/team   ....
- surroundings/neighborhive   ....
....

what will you want to do again with this mission to make your target feel special/that
you made a difference?

....
....

what ideas do you have for your next sting ops mission?

....
....
....

SPEAK UP WITH CONSTRUCTIVE IDEAS AND SOLUTIONS

solo op

61

TARGET: You and the world
TIME: Ongoing
COST: $

MISSION OBJECTIVE:
Be a solution-finding ninja!

GEAR & PROVISIONS:
- Go-get-'em pep in your step
- Ninja vision: problems are opportunities to rise up and win

PREP STEP:
Stay positive. Being optimistic doesn't mean you're pretending challenges don't exist. You just see them as calls to action—opportunities to show what you've got! *Boom!*

GO TIME!
See a challenge and find a way to turn it into a good thing. If nothing else, it's a great learning experience that you can share with others so they don't have to face the same struggle. This could also be your training ground for an amazing opportunity or idea to solve a common problem! Go, ninja!

TACTICAL SUCCESS KEY:
Challenges can make us worry, complain, and feel overwhelmed or scared. Do your best to learn, solve as you go, and ask for help when you need it. Asking for help doesn't make you less of a ninja. We're all in this together! Go team—celebrate the learning!

MY NEIGHBORHIVE MISSION DEBRIEFING
mission completion date ....

how do you feel after completing the sting operation?

....

....

....

what did you notice afterwards?
- about your mission target
- yourself/team
- surroundings/neighborhive

....

....

what will you want to do again with this mission to make your target feel special/that you made a difference?

....

....

....

what ideas do you have for your next sting ops mission?

....

....

....

USE YOUR SKILLS TO HELP FIX SOMETHING FOR A NEIGHBOR

62

solo op or team op

TARGET: Neighbor hiver
TIME: 00:20+
COST: $-$$$

MISSION OBJECTIVE:

Deploy your fix-it skills to help a neighbor hiver with a repair that exceeds his or her abilities.

GEAR & PROVISIONS:

- Clear idea of what needs fixing
- Tools
- Online and other resources to find your solution
- Willingness to bring in a pro, if necessary!

PREP STEP:

Be sure you have a firm understanding of the actual problem (not just its symptoms), especially when dealing with electronics, home plumbing/structural/electrical work, and so on.

GO TIME!

1. Identify the issue, and diagnose the problem.
2. Find a solution, and secure the necessary tools and/or supplies.
3. Fix it—or find someone who can!

TACTICAL SUCCESS KEY:

Sometimes we can help with the knowledge and tools we already have, and other times we need to ask for help. The key to this sting-ops mission is maintaining a solution-finding, get-it-done attitude. Don't hesitate to call in the professionals if you're in over your head.

MY NEIGHBORHIVE MISSION DEBRIEFING
mission completion date ....

how do you feel after completing the sting operation?

....

....

what did you notice afterwards?
- about your mission target
- yourself/team
- surroundings/neighborhive

....

what will you want to do again with this mission to make your target feel special/that you made a difference?

....

....

what ideas do you have for your next sting ops mission?

....

....

....

SUPPORT LOCAL KIDS' SPORTS LEAGUES, ART PROGRAMS, AND ACTIVITIES

solo op or team op

63

TARGET: Local groups for kids' activities

TIME: 00:25+

COST: $-$$$

 MISSION OBJECTIVE:

Get to know your fellow neighbor hivers while also cheering on the youth in your community.

GEAR & PROVISIONS:

- Community activities board and schedule of events
- Money to sponsor, support, or attend activities

☑ PREP STEP:

Do a little research to see if there are specific activity groups you wish to support over others.

🕐 GO TIME!

Decide how you want to support the local kids' programs, and go!

⚲ TACTICAL SUCCESS KEY:

You don't have to choose just one! Try a few different activity groups out once or twice to see if you're inclined to support one or some more than the others.

MY NEIGHBORHIVE MISSION DEBRIEFING
mission completion date ....

how do you feel after completing the sting operation?

....
....

what did you notice afterwards?
- about your mission target
- yourself/team
- surroundings/neighborhive

....

what will you want to do again with this mission to make your target feel special/that you made a difference?

....
....

what ideas do you have for your next sting ops mission?

....
....
....

JOIN A COMMUNITY-SUPPORTED AGRICULTURE (CSA) PROGRAM IN YOUR AREA

solo op or team op

64

TARGET: You and your local farmers
TIME: 00:15+
COST: $$$

🎯 MISSION OBJECTIVE:

Find and join a CSA program near you. Take the opportunity to get to know your farmer!

⚙️ GEAR & PROVISIONS:

- Online resources or local library
- Information from local agricultural groups about CSA availability and opportunities
- Interest in learning about the food you consume by getting to know your local farmer

☑️ PREP STEP:

Visit the farmers' markets in your community, and ask your friends and neighbor hivers about their CSA experiences.

🕐 GO TIME!

1. Research CSA programs.
2. Shop at farmers' markets frequently and ask the farmers you meet about their CSA participation.
3. Enjoy your fresh produce and the adventure of preparing new dishes with it!

🔑 TACTICAL SUCCESS KEY:

Jump on this chance to learn new things about your food and meet some of the growers in your local agricultural community. Some CSA programs even provide workshops and hands-on learning experiences for their members. *Yes!*

MY NEIGHBORHIVE MISSION DEBRIEFING
mission completion date ....

how do you feel after completing the sting operation?

....

....

what did you notice afterwards?
- about your mission target
- yourself/team
- surroundings/neighborhive

....

what will you want to do again with this mission to make your target feel special/that you made a difference?

....

....

what ideas do you have for your next sting ops mission?

....

....

....

TAKE CARE OF YOU

solo op

65

TARGET: You
TIME: Daily
COST: $

MISSION OBJECTIVE:
Bee good to yourself! Take care of you.

GEAR & PROVISIONS:
- Sleep
- Hydration & good food to fuel you
- Physical activity
- Good relationships
- Remembering what connects you to your purpose
- Happy activities (things that make you feel good!)

PREP STEP:
Take good care of yourself, because that's when you can truly give to others and make a difference!

GO TIME!
1. Are there areas in your life that feel unhealthy? How do you want to improve them?

2. What activities are you already doing that you love? Are you able to share those with friends and family?

3. What does your daily routine look like? What do you want to improve so you can get more joy on your daily journey, starting now?

4. Do you know what your goals are? What are you doing to actively pursue them? What could you do on a regular basis to make progress achieving them?

TACTICAL SUCCESS KEY:
Start by adding one or two positive things into your routine, and take it from there. When we show love to ourselves, we can significantly improve our own lives and the lives of those around us by bringing our best selves to the world every day.

MY NEIGHBORHIVE MISSION DEBRIEFING
mission completion date ....

how do you feel after completing the sting operation?

....
....
....

what did you notice afterwards?
* about your mission target   ....
* yourself/team   ....
* surroundings/neighborhive   ....
....

what will you want to do again with this mission to make your target feel special/that you made a difference?

....
....
....

what ideas do you have for your next sting ops mission?

....
....
....

ANONYMOUSLY DO YARD WORK OR SHOVEL SNOW FROM YOUR NEIGHBOR HIVER'S SIDEWALK OR DRIVEWAY WHILE HE OR SHE IS OUT
solo op or team op

66

TARGET: Neighbor hiver
TIME: 00:20+
COST: $

⊚ MISSION OBJECTIVE:
Surprise a neighbor hiver while he or she is out by cleaning up the yard or driveway!

⚙ GEAR & PROVISIONS:
- Serving heart
- Lawn tools or a shovel or snow-blower

☑ PREP STEP:
Know the general time your neighbor hiver will be out, and be sure to take care with his or her property (and no fence hopping or breaking and entering!).

⏱ GO TIME!
Be ready to rock the yard, driveway, or sidewalk once your neighbor hiver steps out. Work with a sense of urgency, and leave no evidence of your ninja identity behind!

⚷ TACTICAL SUCCESS KEY:
Respect your neighbor hiver's point of view and choose a different target if he or she seems troubled by the anonymous efforts. If you don't know your neighbor hiver very well, you may want to sacrifice anonymity and get permission in advance so as to not disrespect him or her while doing your best to brighten the day. Some people already have a service to come take care of these needs, and others like to do the work themselves. Err on the side of caution, and don't take it personally if your neighbor hiver declines your offer to help.

MY NEIGHBORHIVE MISSION DEBRIEFING
mission completion date ....

how do you feel after completing the sting operation?

....
....
....

what did you notice afterwards?
- about your mission target
- yourself/team
- surroundings/neighborhive

....
....
....

what will you want to do again with this mission to make your target feel special/that you made a difference?

....
....
....

what ideas do you have for your next sting ops mission?

....
....
....

ENCOURAGE SOMEONE WHO IS PURSUING A GOAL

solo op or team op

67

TARGET: Friend, family member, child, or neighbor hiver

TIME: 00:05+

COST: $

MISSION OBJECTIVE:

Cheer on a child, friend, or neighbor hiver you know who's focused on pursuing a particular goal.

GEAR & PROVISIONS:

- Genuine, uplifting comments
- Faith that a little "I believe in you!" goes a long way

PREP STEP:

Pursuing a goal at any age is no easy undertaking. Be encouraging and kind!

GO TIME!

1. Select your sting-ops mission target.
2. Ask questions about your target's goal, and be a raving fan!
3. If you wish, make yourself available for future encouragement.

TACTICAL SUCCESS KEY:

This doesn't have to be a big production—positive, encouraging words will be carried around for a lifetime! Let that sink in before you speak, and go onward as someone's personal cheer squad! *Boom!* That's how kindness is done!

MY NEIGHBORHIVE MISSION DEBRIEFING
mission completion date
....

how do you feel after completing the sting operation?
....
....

what did you notice afterwards?
- about your mission target   ....
- yourself/team   ....
- surroundings/neighborhive   ....
....

what will you want to do again with this mission to make your target feel special/that you made a difference?
....
....

what ideas do you have for your next sting ops mission?
....
....

PAY FOR THE PERSON BEHIND YOU AT THE DRIVE-THROUGH

68

solo op or team op

TARGET: Unsuspecting drive-through patron

TIME: 00:05

COST: $-$$$

 MISSION OBJECTIVE:

Conduct a stealth sting op at a drive-through!

GEAR & PROVISIONS:

- Positive energy!
- Gift card or money to cover the order of the person behind you

PREP STEP:

Purchase a gift card in advance of your next visit, or plan to cover the person's order while you pay for yours.

GO TIME!

1. Purchase a gift card in advance, or pay for the order of your sting-ops target when you pay your own.

2. Keep the mission on a need-to-know basis. (Only you and the cashier need to know!)

3. Have a great day!

TACTICAL SUCCESS KEY:

Keep this mission anonymous! Drive off quickly (but safely!) before they catch you, ninja!

MY NEIGHBORHIVE MISSION DEBRIEFING
mission completion date ....

how do you feel after completing the sting operation?

....

....

....

what did you notice afterwards?
- about your mission target
- yourself/team
- surroundings/neighborhive

....

....

....

what will you want to do again with this mission to make your target feel special/that you made a difference?

....

....

....

what ideas do you have for your next sting ops mission?

....

....

....

FILTER YOUR WATER AT HOME AND USE A REUSABLE BOTTLE

69

solo op or team op

TARGET: You and your hivemates
TIME: 00:05
COST: $

MISSION OBJECTIVE:
Hydrate with a purpose! Help your health and the environment, one refreshing sip at a time!

GEAR & PROVISIONS:
- Home water filtration
- Reusable bottle

PREP STEP:
Research the various options for filtering your water at home to find the best option for you.

GO TIME!
1. Filter water.
2. Fill a clean bottle.
3. Hydrate.
4. Repeat. :-)

TACTICAL SUCCESS KEY:
Making a difference in the world doesn't have to take much! It's all about the little things—and they all add up! Do your best to plan ahead to minimize waste and *bee* good to yourself too! Ahhh, now that's the stuff!

MY NEIGHBORHIVE MISSION DEBRIEFING
mission completion date ....

how do you feel after completing the sting operation?

....

....

....

what did you notice afterwards?
- about your mission target
- yourself/team
- surroundings/neighborhive

....

....

....

what will you want to do again with this mission to make your target feel special/that you made a difference?

....

....

....

what ideas do you have for your next sting ops mission?

....

....

....

TUCK A FIVE-DOLLAR BILL INTO A LIBRARY BOOK BEFORE RETURNING IT
solo op or team op

70

TARGET: Your neighborhive library users

TIME: 00:05

COST: $-$$

MISSION OBJECTIVE:
Surprise the next reader of that library book you just finished by tucking a five-dollar bill into it before returning it!

GEAR & PROVISIONS:
- Five-dollar bill(s)
- Library books to return

PREP STEP:
Check out the libraries in your community—and check out some great books to read at the same time.

GO TIME!
1. Visit your local library to check out some books that interest you.

2. Enjoy reading them!

3. Return your library books with a delightful surprise enclosed!

TACTICAL SUCCESS KEY:
Library books get a lot of wear and tear—be gentle, and please avoid using tape or other fasteners that may damage the book. Somewhere in the middle of the pages is the best place for your surprise!

MY NEIGHBORHIVE MISSION DEBRIEFING
mission completion date ....

how do you feel after completing the sting operation?

....
....
....

what did you notice afterwards?
- about your mission target
- yourself/team
- surroundings/neighborhive

....
....

what will you want to do again with this mission to make your target feel special/that you made a difference?

....
....
....

what ideas do you have for your next sting ops mission?

....
....
....

BEE A BUDDY TO NEIGHBORHIVE KIDS

solo op or team op

71

TARGET: Neighborhive kids

TIME: Ongoing, varies

COST: $

🎯 MISSION OBJECTIVE:

Take your neighborhive kids under your wing. The time you spend reading, teaching, and believing in them will make a difference.

⚙️ GEAR & PROVISIONS:

- *Beeing* friendly and respectful of parent or guardian wishes
- A local organization to partner with
- Consistent time to spend with the kids teaching a neat skill, reading, and doing what they enjoy!

☑️ PREP STEP:

Remember that we all need a mentor, coach, or cheer squad to believe in us!

🕐 GO TIME!

1. Partner with a local organization.

2. Commit and follow through on time for *beeing* a buddy.

3. Have a great time reading to, teaching, and encouraging busy bees of all ages!

📍 TACTICAL SUCCESS KEY:

Stay in touch with the parents or guardians of the neighborhive kids you're mentoring. It is important to be respectful of their wishes, including schedule concerns, ongoing expectations, location of activities, and so on. Always talk to your buddy's parents or guardians first before engaging in activities. In some cases, it's best to partner with a local organization that's already laid the groundwork for programs and is connected with families who are interested in participating. Keep up the amazing work in your community!

MY NEIGHBORHIVE MISSION DEBRIEFING
mission completion date

how do you feel after completing the sting operation?

what did you notice afterwards?
- about your mission target
- yourself/team
- surroundings/neighborhive

what will you want to do again with this mission to make your target feel special/that you made a difference?

what ideas do you have for your next sting ops mission?

GIVE NEW OR GENTLY USED TOYS TO A LOCAL WOMEN'S SHELTER

72

solo op or team op

TARGET: Children at a local women's shelter

TIME: 01:30+

COST: $-$$$

MISSION OBJECTIVE:

Brighten the day of kids in a challenging situation by bringing new or gently used toys to a local women's shelter.

GEAR & PROVISIONS:

- Team of stuffed-toy donors and collectors
- Bags and boxes
- Local women's shelter ready to accept the toys

PREP STEP:

Call local women's shelters to inform them of your intent. Ask if there are specific donation guidelines or restrictions to be aware of before beginning the process.

GO TIME!

1. Check in with the administrators at a local women's shelter about providing donated stuffed toys. Also, consider partnering with local charitable or service organizations to maximize your efforts.

2. Have your team ask friends and family members to gather stuffed toys, and then collect them.

3. Deliver the donations to the local women's shelter you've partnered with.

TACTICAL SUCCESS KEY:

Clarify any regulations pertaining to stuffed-toy donations at your local women's shelter (some will only accept new toys for health and safety reasons). Seek out local organizations you can partner with to maximize your stuffed-toy drive. After you've gathered the plush bounty, be sure the donations are appropriately distributed. Happy stinging!

MY NEIGHBORHIVE MISSION DEBRIEFING
mission completion date ....

how do you feel after completing the sting operation?

....

....

....

what did you notice afterwards?
- about your mission target
- yourself/team
- surroundings/neighborhive

....

....

what will you want to do again with this mission to make your target feel special/that you made a difference?

....

....

....

what ideas do you have for your next sting ops mission?

....

....

....

PRACTICE KINDNESS TOWARD A HOMELESS PERSON

73

solo op or team op

TARGET: Homeless person in your community

TIME: 00:35+

COST: $-$$

MISSION OBJECTIVE:

Bring a little sunshine to a homeless person by sharing some coffee and conversation.

GEAR & PROVISIONS:

- Smile and a friendly attitude!
- Beverage(s) or treat(s)

PREP STEP:

These folks are spending their days in very difficult conditions and situations, so be ready to go into this sting-ops mission with a friendly smile and a genuine spirit of "You matter to me." That will go a long way!

GO TIME!

1. Have your smile, authenticity, and beverage or snack ready to spread some sunshine.

2. Remember to introduce yourself.

3. Then spend a little time getting to know him or her.

TACTICAL SUCCESS KEY:

Take extra care with these wonderful people; they have braved so much and have so little. People become homeless for many different reasons, so it's important to be sensitive to who they are and what they may have been through without being judgmental. Your amazing spirit is sure to brighten their day and give them hope for a better tomorrow. Thank you for accepting this mission and completing it with dignity and respect for those less fortunate in the community.

MY NEIGHBORHIVE MISSION DEBRIEFING
mission completion date ....

how do you feel after completing the sting operation?

....

....

what did you notice afterwards?
- about your mission target ....
- yourself/team ....
- surroundings/neighborhive ....

....

what will you want to do again with this mission to make your target feel special/that you made a difference?

....

....

what ideas do you have for your next sting ops mission?

....

....

....

HELP SOMEONE IN YOUR NEIGHBORHIVE WHO MAY NEED ASSISTANCE WITH GROCERY SHOPPING AND UNPACKING PURCHASES AT HOME
solo op or team op

74

TARGET: Fellow neighbor hiver (the elderly, busy parent, etc.)

TIME: 01:00+

COST: $

MISSION OBJECTIVE:
Ninja grocery-store move! *Pow!*

GEAR & PROVISIONS:
- Smile and a "how can I be helpful?" attitude
- Transportation
- Special accommodations for your neighbor hiver, if necessary
- Your mission target's shopping list

☑ PREP STEP:
Take time to get to know your neighbor hiver, and ask him or her the best ways you can help.

⏱ GO TIME!
1. Ask about specific ways you can help and determine a date and time to do so.
2. Help with grocery shopping, errands, and so on.
3. Deliver and unpack groceries; put them away for your neighbor hiver, if he or she consents.

⚷ TACTICAL SUCCESS KEY:
Keep in mind that people move at different paces, so plan extra time as a cushion for yourself. Some challenges may come along with this sting-ops mission, but your fellow neighbor hiver really appreciates you, whether or not he or she expresses it.

MY NEIGHBORHIVE MISSION DEBRIEFING
mission completion date ....

how do you feel after completing the sting operation?

....

....

....

what did you notice afterwards?
- about your mission target   ....
- yourself/team   ....
- surroundings/neighborhive   ....

....

....

what will you want to do again with this mission to make your target feel special/that you made a difference?

....

....

....

what ideas do you have for your next sting ops mission?

....

....

....

MINIMIZE EXTRA DRIVING AND AIR POLLUTION BY PLANNING OUT YOUR ERRANDS IN ADVANCE

solo op or team op

75

TARGET: You and your neighborhive air

TIME: Varies

COST: $

MISSION OBJECTIVE:

Consolidate your errands and strategize your route carefully to reduce air pollution.

GEAR & PROVISIONS:

- Ninja time-management skills
- Your to-do list and schedule

PREP STEP:

You're keeping the air around you cleaner while also saving yourself time and fuel costs by planning your trips in advance!

GO TIME!

1. Divide your to-do list by location and estimate time at each stop.

2. Chunk out time in your schedule for errands.

3. Assign grouped tasks by location to a time slot that fits by priority and duration.

TACTICAL SUCCESS KEY:

Partner with a friend who has similar errands so you can carpool or divide and conquer tasks by helping each other out! Every trip you save means cleaner air to breathe for everyone in your community! You're awesome!

MY NEIGHBORHIVE MISSION DEBRIEFING
mission completion date ....

how do you feel after completing the sting operation?

....
....
....

what did you notice afterwards?
- about your mission target
- yourself/team
- surroundings/neighborhive

....
....

what will you want to do again with this mission to make your target feel special/that you made a difference?

....
....
....

what ideas do you have for your next sting ops mission?

....
....
....

PARTICIPATE IN SOMETHING YOU'VE NEVER DONE TO MAKE NEW FRIENDS

solo op or team op

76

TARGET: You
TIME: 01:00+
COST: $-$$$

🎯 MISSION OBJECTIVE:
Do something new!

⚙️ GEAR & PROVISIONS:
- Willingness to do an activity you haven't tried before
- Open mind and heart to new people
- List of different activities you've always wanted to do—or even things you've never considered

☑️ PREP STEP:
Don't prejudge people or activities—keep an open mind and have a good time.

🕐 GO TIME!
1. Take a look at your list of new and untried activities. Pick one!
2. Do it, introduce yourself to others, and have a blast!

🔑 TACTICAL SUCCESS KEY:
You're one brave ninja for stepping into the unknown like this! By taking leaps of faith and learning to not be afraid of new and different things, you're much better prepared for other new experiences—both challenges and triumphs! Awesome!

MY NEIGHBORHIVE MISSION DEBRIEFING
mission completion date

how do you feel after completing the sting operation?

what did you notice afterwards?
- about your mission target
- yourself/team
- surroundings/neighborhive

what will you want to do again with this mission to make your target feel special/that you made a difference?

what ideas do you have for your next sting ops mission?

BUY ONLY WHAT YOU NEED; DON'T WASTE

solo op or team op

77

TARGET: You, others, your neighborhive

TIME: Varies, ongoing

COST: $

MISSION OBJECTIVE:
Reduce waste.

GEAR & PROVISIONS:
- Mindful purchasing
- Online consumer resources
- Openness to identifying wasteful items that can be eliminated or replaced by something recyclable or reusable

PREP STEP:
Evaluate your purchasing and consumption habits and find ways to improve your shopping and usage habits.

GO TIME!
1. Evaluate your current purchasing and consumption habits.
2. Take concrete steps to improve your shopping and usage habits.
3. Keep up the momentum as you reduce waste! Share what you learn with others!

TACTICAL SUCCESS KEY:
Begin with one or two changes, and make small adjustments as you go. Every bit counts, and small progress is still progress! Build on that, and your new habits will be much more sustainable as you move forward. Oh yeah!

MY NEIGHBORHIVE MISSION DEBRIEFING
mission completion date ....

how do you feel after completing the sting operation?

....

....

....

what did you notice afterwards?
- about your mission target ....
- yourself/team ....
- surroundings/neighborhive ....

....

what will you want to do again with this mission to make your target feel special/that you made a difference?

....

....

....

what ideas do you have for your next sting ops mission?

....

....

....

GET A PEN PAL AND SEND SOME LONG-DISTANCE SUNSHINE

78

solo op or team op

TARGET: Pen pal, friend, or relative
TIME: 00:25+
COST: $-$$$

MISSION OBJECTIVE:
Use the mail system to carry some sunshine far and wide.

GEAR & PROVISIONS:
- A sting-ops mission target
- Note card, box, and postage
- Mailing address
- A small treat, book, trinket, and the like as a small "thinking of you" gesture to spread the sunshine!

PREP STEP:
Everyone loves to receive unexpected good things! Keep it simple—it truly is the thought that counts!

GO TIME!
1. Shop for a little something, keeping your target's likes in mind.
2. Write a thoughtful note to include with the package.
3. Pack it, seal it, ship it off!

TACTICAL SUCCESS KEY:
Don't go too crazy on purchases. Something small makes just as big an impact as something large or expensive. If your target is traveling, a smaller item is better for portability. The less you spend on each sting-ops target, the more long-distance sunshine you can send to others who need it too!

MY NEIGHBORHIVE MISSION DEBRIEFING
mission completion date ....

how do you feel after completing the sting operation?

....

....

....

what did you notice afterwards?

- about your mission target   ....

- yourself/team   ....

- surroundings/neighborhive   ....

....

....

what will you want to do again with this mission to make your target feel special/that you made a difference?

....

....

....

what ideas do you have for your next sting ops mission?

....

....

....

LEARN ANOTHER LANGUAGE, AND THEN PRACTICE WITH SOMEONE WHO SPEAKS IT AS A FIRST LANGUAGE
solo op

79

TARGET: You

TIME: Varies

COST: $-$$$

MISSION OBJECTIVE:

Expand your cultural horizons by studying a new language, and then find a willing native speaker so you can practice your new skills.

GEAR & PROVISIONS:

- Patience with yourself and the learning process
- Language-learning software, course, tutor, or other resources
- A place to practice speaking the language you're learning

PREP STEP:

Think about which languages interest you and why. That will help you stay motivated during any road bumps in the learning process.

GO TIME!

1. Pick a language to learn.
2. Secure your language-learning tools or resources (e.g., enroll in a course).
3. Practice, practice, practice!

TACTICAL SUCCESS KEY:

Learning another language is an amazing way to grow and see the world through new eyes. It also offers you a new way to connect with others who speak that language!

MY NEIGHBORHIVE MISSION DEBRIEFING
mission completion date _____

how do you feel after completing the sting operation?

....

....

....

what did you notice afterwards?
- about your mission target
- yourself/team
- surroundings/neighborhive

....

what will you want to do again with this mission to make your target feel special/that you made a difference?

....

....

....

what ideas do you have for your next sting ops mission?

....

....

....

159

RECYCLE AND UPCYCLE

80

solo op or team op

TARGET: Your home and neighborhive

TIME: Ongoing, varies

COST: $-$$$

MISSION OBJECTIVE:

Find ways to give new life to the old or unused objects around you. Recycle and upcycle by asking, "How can I repurpose this instead of throwing it away?"

GEAR & PROVISIONS:

- Ninja ingenuity (a.k.a. *ninja*nuity!)
- Local recycling program

PREP STEP:

Be mindful of what you might be wasting, and think of ways to reuse items that otherwise would go to the trash.

GO TIME!

1. Use your local recycling program.

2. Seek out ways to repurpose items that don't decompose or can't be recycled.

TACTICAL SUCCESS KEY:

Take advantage of the many online resources that provide strategies to reduce your footprint and ways to repurpose what you already have for crafts, home improvement, home decor, and the like. Have fun on your recycle/upcycle adventure—and explore how to change your buying habits to avoid purchasing harmful materials. Every little bit counts, so keep up the great work!

MY NEIGHBORHIVE MISSION DEBRIEFING
mission completion date ....

how do you feel after completing the sting operation?

....

....

what did you notice afterwards?
- about your mission target
- yourself/team
- surroundings/neighborhive

what will you want to do again with this mission to make your target feel special/that you made a difference?

....

....

what ideas do you have for your next sting ops mission?

....

....

....

UPLIFT AND CELEBRATE DIFFERENCES AND UNCOMMON ABILITIES
solo op

81

TARGET: Anyone around you
TIME: Daily
COST: $

MISSION OBJECTIVE:
Recognize and applaud the singular attributes and achievements of those around you—and avoid the trap of making comparisons.

GEAR & PROVISIONS:
- Attitude of gratitude
- Ninja vision to see others' superpowers!

PREP STEP:
How boring would life be if we were all the same? Everyone adds value, and differences are a good thing! We all help each other grow. We can all learn something new from someone else. Life's not a competition, it's an adventure!

GO TIME!
1. Practice gratitude every day, recognizing what others have helped teach you by sharing their different life experiences.

2. Acknowledge others' unique contributions: Tell them how awesome they are! Doing this on a regular basis will greatly improve your ninja vision and encourage them too!

TACTICAL SUCCESS KEY:
People know when you're sugarcoating stuff, and that isn't helpful to anyone. At first this might feel uncomfortable, but with practice you'll be one of the most skilled ninjas out there, spreading sunshine in your own awesome way. Stay genuine, positive, and caring (*bee* the real deal). *Boom!*

MY NEIGHBORHIVE MISSION DEBRIEFING
mission completion date ....

how do you feel after completing the sting operation?

....
....
....

what did you notice afterwards?
- about your mission target
- yourself/team
- surroundings/neighborhive

....
....
....
....

what will you want to do again with this mission to make your target feel special/that you made a difference?

....
....
....

what ideas do you have for your next sting ops mission?

....
....
....

ENJOY MORE MEATLESS MEALS WITH YOUR FAMILY ON A REGULAR BASIS
solo op or team op

82

TARGET: You and your hivemates
TIME: 00:35+
COST: $-$$

MISSION OBJECTIVE:
Minimize the meat!

GEAR & PROVISIONS:
- Menu-planning resources
- Shopping list
- Enthusiastic (or at least willing) taste testers

PREP STEP:
Plan your meals in advance to optimize nutritional—and flavor—content!

GO TIME!
1. Use online resources for meal ideas and planning.
2. Incorporate the menu ingredients into your household shopping list.
3. Experiment with different meatless recipes, and enjoy the flavor adventure!

TACTICAL SUCCESS KEY:
Have an open mind when it comes to meatless cuisine. The new recipes you try may not become your new favorites, but cooking different foods or in different ways expands your horizons and increases your appreciation for your tried-and-true dishes. And who knows, you may discover the next best meatless meal!

MY NEIGHBORHIVE MISSION DEBRIEFING
mission completion date
....

how do you feel after completing the sting operation?

....

....

....

what did you notice afterwards?
- about your mission target ....
- yourself/team ....
- surroundings/neighborhive ....

....

what will you want to do again with this mission to make your target feel special/that you made a difference?

....

....

....

what ideas do you have for your next sting ops mission?

....

....

....

START A COMMUNITY GARDEN

83

team op

TARGET: Your neighborhive—its people and its pollinators!

TIME: 02:00+

COST: $$$

🎯 MISSION OBJECTIVE:

Bring a vacant lot back to life by starting a community garden to share the beauty of growing food with your neighbor hivers and pollinators!

⚙️ GEAR & PROVISIONS:

- Location for a community garden (e.g., a vacant lot, etc.)
- Seeds and plants that are good for you and your local pollinators
- A care plan so the team knows who will feed, weed, and water, and when those things should get done

☑️ PREP STEP:

If you're looking at a vacant lot or a shared public area to start your garden, be sure to check with local regulating authorities to make sure it's a community-approved site. If the site you were scoping isn't compliant, keep looking and find another option that will be approved. Visit your local home-improvement store and garden center for information on how to build your garden.

🕐 GO TIME!

1. Finalize the location and the sting-ops team.

2. Plan your garden: Select seeds and plants th are friendly to people and local pollinators.

3. Create a care plan to strategize who will do what and when. Enjoy—and happy gardening

🔑 TACTICAL SUCCESS KEY:

Use online resources to find plants that will work best in your area and learn tips for creating a thriving and productive community garden! Consider working with local organizations or companies th specialize in community gardens so you can keep the focus on having fun with the project and your fellow neighbor hivers while also following local laws and regulations. That's a win for everyone!

MY NEIGHBORHIVE MISSION DEBRIEFING
mission completion date

how do you feel after completing the sting operation?

....

....

what did you notice afterwards?
- about your mission target
- yourself/team
- surroundings/neighborhive

....

....

what will you want to do again with this mission to make your target feel special/that you made a difference?

....

....

what ideas do you have for your next sting ops mission?

....

....

ORGANIZE FAMILY VOLUNTEERING OPPORTUNITIES IN ADDITION TO ENTERTAINMENT ACTIVITIES LIKE MOVIES OR THEME PARKS
team op

84

TARGET: Your family

TIME: 01:30+

COST: $-$$$

🎯 MISSION OBJECTIVE:
Volunteer activities as a family!

⚙️ GEAR & PROVISIONS:
- Service-oriented mentality
- Local organizations to volunteer for as a family unit
- Time to volunteer
- Time to talk about the experience afterward

☑️ PREP STEP:
Have an ongoing conversation with your family about the importance of being a good citizen in the community and giving back when possible. Ask your kids for their input on what types of causes they'd like to help support.

🕐 GO TIME!
1. Connect with a local organization that needs volunteers.
2. Talk about it with family and set aside the time.
3. Get excited and have fun while you give back to the community.
4. Talk about the experience afterward to share what you all learned and how you feel about the experience.

🔑 TACTICAL SUCCESS KEY:
This mission is about doing things you haven't done before and adding value in the community where you can. Explore a variety of different volunteer activities with your family and talk about it frequently. You may discover new opportunities to make a difference when and where you least expect them!

MY NEIGHBORHIVE MISSION DEBRIEFING
mission completion date

how do you feel after completing the sting operation?

what did you notice afterwards?
- about your mission target
- yourself/team
- surroundings/neighborhive

what will you want to do again with this mission to make your target feel special/that you made a difference?

what ideas do you have for your next sting ops mission?

ANONYMOUSLY PAY FOR SOMEONE'S GROCERIES

solo op or team op

85

TARGET: Unsuspecting person or family

TIME: 00:05

COST: $$–$$$

MISSION OBJECTIVE:

Surprise an individual or a family by taking care of a food purchase behind the scenes.

GEAR & PROVISIONS:

- Positive energy!
- Gift card for a grocery store

PREP STEP:

Purchase a gift card to the grocery store as you check out. Give it to a cashier to use for another shopper right away or save it for your next visit. Either way, remain undetected!

GO TIME!

1. Purchase a grocery-store gift card.

2. Quietly disclose to the cashier that you'd like to use it for the shopper two people behind you, or ask him or her to take the card to another cashier after you leave and apply it to a customer checking out in that line.

3. Keep it under wraps!

TACTICAL SUCCESS KEY:

Remember this is a top-secret, anonymous sting op. Everybody eats, and they've already picked out what they want! Spread some sunshine in a grocery cart!

MY NEIGHBORHIVE MISSION DEBRIEFING
mission completion date ....

how do you feel after completing the sting operation?

....

....

what did you notice afterwards?
- about your mission target
- yourself/team
- surroundings/neighborhive

....

....

what will you want to do again with this mission to make your target feel special/that you made a difference?

....

....

what ideas do you have for your next sting ops mission?

....

....

SEND LETTERS OF ENCOURAGEMENT

86

solo op or team op

TARGET: Deployed troops
TIME: 00:05+
COST: $-$$

⊚ MISSION OBJECTIVE:
Send letters of encouragement to those serving our country away from home.

⚙ GEAR & PROVISIONS:
- Contact information or mailing address
- Note cards or stationery and postage stamps

☑ PREP STEP:
Think about those making sacrifices in service to others, and consider what you want to say to thank them. Then send them some long-distance sunshine!

⊕ GO TIME!
1. Select your mission target (a.k.a. card recipient).
2. Write a thoughtful and genuine note.
3. Send it off with some sunshine and positive energy!

⚷ TACTICAL SUCCESS KEY:
Get in touch with an armed forces' local administrative office for details on how and where to send your notes. They can be whatever length feels natural to you. Focus on thanking and cheering up the service member who will receive your note. As long as you use your authentic voice and speak from the heart, your mission will be a success!

MY NEIGHBORHIVE MISSION DEBRIEFING
mission completion date
....

how do you feel after completing the sting operation?

....
....
....

what did you notice afterwards?
- about your mission target
- yourself/team
- surroundings/neighborhive

....
....
....

what will you want to do again with this mission to make your target feel special/that you made a difference?

....
....
....

what ideas do you have for your next sting ops mission?

....
....
....

BRING A BEVERAGE TO YOUR GARBAGE-REMOVAL TEAM

solo op or team op

87

TARGET: Sanitation worker

TIME: 00:05

COST: $

MISSION OBJECTIVE:

Bring a refreshing beverage to your garbage-removal team (e.g., lemonade or a soda in warm weather, and coffee or hot cocoa when it's cold). They work hard and deserve your appreciation.

GEAR & PROVISIONS:

- Smile!
- Beverage(s)

PREP STEP:

These folks are working very hard in rough conditions. A friendly smile and your effort to brighten their day will go a very long way! The best prep is knowing the general time they'll arrive so you won't miss them or put them behind schedule.

GO TIME!

Have your winning attitude, smile, and beverages ready to rock—and then deliver!

TACTICAL SUCCESS KEY:

Keep in mind that neighborhive maintenance workers are on the job, sometimes on a very tight time line (without much time to chat), and may not be able to accept your act of kindness for reasons they don't decide (company policy, local regulations, etc.). This is about spreading the sunshine, so even if they decline, wish them a great day (and try to do the same yourself)!

MY NEIGHBORHIVE MISSION DEBRIEFING
mission completion date ....

how do you feel after completing the sting operation?

....

....

....

what did you notice afterwards?
- about your mission target
- yourself/team
- surroundings/neighborhive

....

....

what will you want to do again with this mission to make your target feel special/that you made a difference?

....

....

....

what ideas do you have for your next sting ops mission?

....

....

....

CULTIVATE A POLLINATOR GARDEN IN THE COMMUNITY

88

solo op or team op

TARGET: Pollinators in your neighborhive

TIME: 01:30+

COST: $-$$$

MISSION OBJECTIVE:

Create a garden in the community designed especially for your pollinator pals!

GEAR & PROVISIONS:

- Proper location in your neighborhive
- Sunlight-exposed area for plants and flowers
- Healthy soil
- Seeds and plants that are friendly to area pollinators
- Online resources to help you plan and care for your bee retreat
- Time to commit to regularly feed, water, and weed
- Bee-break hydration station

☑ PREP STEP:

Research what plants and flowers your local pollinators eat so you can focus on designing your garden around them.

GO TIME!

1. Research your local bees and pollinators to discover what they eat.
2. Plan and plant your garden.
3. Water, feed, and weed your garden regularly.
4. Buzz with satisfaction as you watch your garden grow!

TACTICAL SUCCESS KEY:

After you finish planning and planting, be sure to find consistent time to care for the plants. If bees visit you as you're tending to their garden buffet, please be gentle and don't swat them away. Bees sting if they feel threatened or alarmed, so either calmly keep caring for your garden, or come back to it at another time.

MY NEIGHBORHIVE MISSION DEBRIEFING
mission completion date

how do you feel after completing the sting operation?

what did you notice afterwards?
- about your mission target
- yourself/team
- surroundings/neighborhive

what will you want to do again with this mission to make your target feel special/that you made a difference?

what ideas do you have for your next sting ops mission?

SHUT OFF SOCIAL MEDIA FOR A WEEK AND GO MEET PEOPLE IN YOUR COMMUNITY

solo op or team op

89

TARGET: You and others

TIME: One week

COST: $

MISSION OBJECTIVE:

Unplug to connect in person!

GEAR & PROVISIONS:

- Open mind
- Activities to meet neighbor hivers
- A positive replacement activity to do when you feel the urge to plug back in

PREP STEP:

Let your friends and family know in advance how to reach you during your seven-day break from the digital world (if the way you normally stay in touch is through social media).

GO TIME!

1. Keep an open mind—and hang in there!

2. Plan activities with other people, those you know and some you don't yet know.

3. Replace the urge to plug in with a different fun activity.

TACTICAL SUCCESS KEY:

This mission can be a challenge to some for many different reasons. It is difficult to break habits, and though you will likely go back to using social media after the week, you'll become much more aware of your usage (as well as others'). You have so much to offer the world offline—explore that. The cyberhive will still be there when you're ready to return to it.

MY NEIGHBORHIVE MISSION DEBRIEFING
mission completion date

how do you feel after completing the sting operation?

what did you notice afterwards?
- about your mission target
- yourself/team
- surroundings/neighborhive

what will you want to do again with this mission to make your target feel special/that you made a difference?

what ideas do you have for your next sting ops mission?

DONATE STUFFED ANIMALS FOR KIDS WHO HAVE TO RIDE IN AN AMBULANCE OR POLICE CAR

team op

90

TARGET: Local children

TIME: 01:30+

COST: $$-$$$

MISSION OBJECTIVE:

Bring some stuffed-toy comfort to children who have to go on an ambulance or police car ride.

GEAR & PROVISIONS:

- Team of stuffed-toy donors and collectors
- Bags or boxes
- Local police or fire department organization to accept the donated stuffed toys

PREP STEP:

Call your local police or fire department administration to inform them of your intent and to see if there are specific policies or practices to be aware of before beginning the collection process.

GO TIME!

1. Check in with your local police or fire department administration before you begin.

2. Consider partnering with a local organization.

3. Have the sting-ops team ask friends and family members to gather stuffed toys.

4. Collect the toys, and deliver them as planned.

TACTICAL SUCCESS KEY:

Check with local police and fire department administrations to clarify any regulations about stuffed-toy donations. (Some will require brand-new toys and will be unable to accept gently used toys for health and safety reasons.) Partnering with local service organizations can maximize your efforts and help ensure the donations are appropriately distributed. Have fun, and happy stinging!

MY NEIGHBORHIVE MISSION DEBRIEFING
mission completion date ....

how do you feel after completing the sting operation?

....
....

what did you notice afterwards?
- about your mission target
- yourself/team
- surroundings/neighborhive

....

what will you want to do again with this mission to make your target feel special/that you made a difference?

....
....

what ideas do you have for your next sting ops mission?

....
....
....

VOLUNTEER TO READ TO OR SPEND TIME WITH RESIDENTS OF A NURSING HOME OR HOSPICE
solo op or team op

91

TARGET: Elderly neighbor hivers
TIME: 01:00+
COST: $

 MISSION OBJECTIVE:
Bring joy and delight to residents of a nursing home or hospice by volunteering to read to and spend time with them!

GEAR & PROVISIONS:
- Smile, friendly attitude, and spirit of fun
- Local organization(s) to partner with
- A variety of options to read (if the residents don't have their own materials)

PREP STEP:
These folks may be feeling aches and pains that can come with older age, loneliness, and other hurts they might not want to discuss. Come alongside them with tender care and kindness. You will gain so much from completing this mission!

GO TIME!
1. Partner with a local elder-care organization, nursing home, or hospice to determine how you can help encourage residents by reading to or spending time with them.

2. Commit time to volunteering and follow through.

3. Enjoy the company of your new friend(s) as you give them the care and attention they deserve!

TACTICAL SUCCESS KEY:
This mission is especially rewarding, but there can be challenges as well. Be sure to communicate with the staff of the organization or home you're visiting to have a better understanding of how to support the resident in a way that works best for him or her. You're such a brilliant ray of sunshine!

MY NEIGHBORHIVE MISSION DEBRIEFING
mission completion date

how do you feel after completing the sting operation?

what did you notice afterwards?
- about your mission target
- yourself/team
- surroundings/neighborhive

what will you want to do again with this mission to make your target feel special/that you made a difference?

what ideas do you have for your next sting ops mission?

HELP THE ELDERLY LEARN HOW TO CONNECT TO FRIENDS AND FAMILY USING THE INTERNET
solo op or team op

92

TARGET: Elderly neighbor hiver

TIME: 00:35+

COST: $

MISSION OBJECTIVE:
Share some of the benefits of the digital world by teaching an elderly person how to connect to family members and friends using the Internet.

GEAR & PROVISIONS:
- Patience
- Spirit of fun!
- A local organization as a partner to connect you with your elderly neighbor hivers

PREP STEP:
Think about how great it will be for an elderly person to finally see up-to-date pictures of long-distance family members online once they know how to access them!

GO TIME!
1. Locate places to go to help your new friend learn how to use the Internet and hang out with him or her.
2. Take time to get to know your target, and stay focused on having a great time with him or her.
3. If you end up ditching the Internet thing, that's great too!

TACTICAL SUCCESS KEY:
It can be challenging for anyone to learn a new skill set, so it's essential to be patient with your new friend. Keep it fun and stress-free. If he or she doesn't want to continue learning the ins and outs of a digital presence, don't worry. Talk about something else, or go do another activity with him or her. Keep it relaxed, and you'll both enjoy the process.

MY NEIGHBORHIVE MISSION DEBRIEFING
mission completion date ....

how do you feel after completing the sting operation?

....

....

what did you notice afterwards?
- about your mission target
- yourself/team
- surroundings/neighborhive

what will you want to do again with this mission to make your target feel special/that you made a difference?

....

....

what ideas do you have for your next sting ops mission?

....

....

....

HELP A LOCAL FARMER WITH CHORES FOR A DAY

93

solo op or team op

TARGET: Local farmer, you
TIME: Varies
COST: $

MISSION OBJECTIVE:

Pitch in and help a local farmer complete his or her daily chores.

GEAR & PROVISIONS:

- Agreement with farmer
- Good work shoes or boots and work clothes
- Hydration!
- Willingness to learn and serve

PREP STEP:

✓ Reach out to area farmers or agricultural organizations to see if there are current or future opportunities to help out for a day.

GO TIME!

1. Connect with an area farmer or agricultural organization to seek out volunteer opportunities.

2. Follow guidelines; be prepared for hard work; and stay flexible and eager to help.

3. Think about what you learned. Did anything change in how you view farming or food?

TACTICAL SUCCESS KEY:

In some areas, helping out a farmer in this capacity isn't possible, but you can still explore agricultural learning with a hands-on experience through other groups or organizations. Keep seeking opportunities to learn and help!

MY NEIGHBORHIVE MISSION DEBRIEFING
mission completion date

how do you feel after completing the sting operation?

what did you notice afterwards?
- about your mission target
- yourself/team
- surroundings/neighborhive

what will you want to do again with this mission to make your target feel special/that you made a difference?

what ideas do you have for your next sting ops mission?

ORGANIZE A NEIGHBORHOOD OUTDOOR FOOD AND MUSIC OR MOVIE NIGHT
team op

94

TARGET: Your neighbor hivers
TIME: 01:30
COST: $$–$$$

MISSION OBJECTIVE:
Host a fun gathering for your neighbor hivers to connect in the outdoors!

GEAR & PROVISIONS:
- Event location
- Event invites (online or hard copy)
- Reasonable budget
- Menu plan and shopping list
- Neighborhive-friendly music and movies, and/or live musicians and audiovisual equipment
- To-do list that outlines who's doing what and when, including a prep and event time line

PREP STEP:
Find a date and time that works for most people and that will allow enough time for your team to prepare for the event. Great planning will make it enjoyable for everyone!

GO TIME!
1. Gather your sting-ops team and strategize responsibilities—divvy them up and agree on timing to complete the tasks.
2. Plan the date, time, and location, and then invite your fellow neighbor hivers out for a great time! (They may also want to help with the event, so think about how to respond when excited invitees ask how they can help.)
3. Keep track of your to-do list, and work to steadily check things off as the event approaches. (Ask for help when you need it!)
4. Host the event, and have a great time!

TACTICAL SUCCESS KEY:
Remember, it's about having fun and connecting with your neighbor hivers. Don't overthink it, and enjoy supporting others' ideas in the planning process.

MY NEIGHBORHIVE MISSION DEBRIEFING
mission completion date ....

how do you feel after completing the sting operation?

....

....

what did you notice afterwards?
- about your mission target
- yourself/team
- surroundings/neighborhive

....

....

....

....

what will you want to do again with this mission to make your target feel special/that you made a difference?

....

....

....

what ideas do you have for your next sting ops mission?

....

....

....

BLES*STING* SOMEONE WITH A SUNNY NOTE

solo op

95

TARGET: Unsuspecting friend, family member, coworker, classmate, or random neighbor hiver

TIME: 00:05

COST: $

MISSION OBJECTIVE:

Brighten someone's day with a note of praise and encouragement (e.g., "You're awesome. Keep shining!")

GEAR & PROVISIONS:

- Ninja vision and stealthy sting-ops skills
- Paper, a card, or a sticky note on which to write your cheery message

PREP STEP:

Notice someone who could use a little sunshine, and find the best time to sneak an encouraging note into his or her day!

GO TIME!

1. Pick your sting-ops target.
2. Write a brief and anonymous note of encouragement.
3. Leave the note where your target will find it easily but won't be able to otherwise detect your visit or determine the source of the mystery praise. Go, ninja, go!

TACTICAL SUCCESS KEY:

This is a note of encouragement, so be appropriate and tactful in your approach. Be sure you're not trespassing or invading your target's privacy or personal space when you conduct your sting-ops delivery. Keep it simple, keep it sunny!

MY NEIGHBORHIVE MISSION DEBRIEFING
mission completion date ....

how do you feel after completing the sting operation?

....

....

....

what did you notice afterwards?
- about your mission target
- yourself/team
- surroundings/neighborhive

....

....

what will you want to do again with this mission to make your target feel special/that
you made a difference?

....

....

....

what ideas do you have for your next sting ops mission?

....

....

....

SURPRISE YOUR NEIGHBORS WITH A HOMEMADE TREAT

96

solo op or team op

TARGET: Your neighbor hivers
TIME: 00:30+
COST: $-$$

MISSION OBJECTIVE:

Deliver a homemade (store-bought is fine, too!) treat to surprise your neighbors.

GEAR & PROVISIONS:

- Smile!
- The goodies

PREP STEP:

Be aware of any allergies or dietary restrictions, if possible. If any common allergens are in your goodies (e.g., nuts), please be kind and leave a note that indicates which ones, just in case.

GO TIME!

1. Have your winning attitude, smile, and treats ready to rock—then deliver!

2. For this sting-ops mission, it's OK to leave anonymity behind. Since you're delivering food, you want to let them know the source! We all want to be safe about what we consume.

TACTICAL SUCCESS KEY:

Keep in mind that your neighbor hiver may not be able to accept your act of kindness for reasons he or she won't disclose—and that's just fine! This is about spreading the sunshine, so even if your neighbor hiver declines, you are still bringing sunshine to his or her day!

MY NEIGHBORHIVE MISSION DEBRIEFING
mission completion date

how do you feel after completing the sting operation?

what did you notice afterwards?
- about your mission target
- yourself/team
- surroundings/neighborhive

what will you want to do again with this mission to make your target feel special/that you made a difference?

what ideas do you have for your next sting ops mission?

EXPLORE NEW DISHES WITH FOODS AND FLAVORS YOU'VE NEVER TASTED BEFORE

solo op or team op

97

TARGET: You and your hivemates

TIME: 00:35+

COST: $-$$$

MISSION OBJECTIVE:

Expand your horizons—and boost the variety in your diet—by experimenting with new recipes and ingredients.

GEAR & PROVISIONS:

- Menu-planning resources
- Shopping list
- Taste testers!

PREP STEP:

Plan your meals in advance to optimize nutritional (and flavor!) content.

GO TIME!

1. Use online resources for recipe ideas and meal planning.

2. Incorporate the recipe ingredients into your household shopping list.

3. Experiment with a variety of new recipes.

4. Enjoy the flavor adventure!

TACTICAL SUCCESS KEY:

Have an open mind when it comes to new cuisine. Preparing new foods or familiar ingredients in different ways builds your food know-how and expands your culinary repertoire. You may make some surprising discoveries, even if it is only the new experience or making new friends in the process!

MY NEIGHBORHIVE MISSION DEBRIEFING
mission completion date ....

how do you feel after completing the sting operation?

....

....

....

what did you notice afterwards?
- about your mission target   ....
- yourself/team
- surroundings/neighborhive   ....

....

what will you want to do again with this mission to make your target feel special/that
you made a difference?

....

....

....

what ideas do you have for your next sting ops mission?

....

....

....

ENJOY DAYS WITHOUT YOUR CELL PHONE, COMPUTER, AND TV

98

solo op

TARGET: You
TIME: Varies, ongoing
COST: $

🎯 MISSION OBJECTIVE:
Screen your screen time.

⚙️ GEAR & PROVISIONS:
- Open mind
- Activities to help you meet your neighbor hivers
- A positive replacement activity to do when you feel the urge for screen time

☑️ PREP STEP:
Tell your friends and family your plan in advance, and give them another way to reach you if they need you.

🕐 GO TIME!
1. Keep an open mind, and hang in there!
2. Plan activities with other people—those you know and some you don't know yet.
3. Replace the urge to plug in with a different activity.

🔑 TACTICAL SUCCESS KEY:
This mission can be a challenge to some of us for many different reasons. It's difficult to break habits—but by setting aside your devices for a time, you'll become much more aware of your own technology usage (as well as others' tech dependence). You have so much to offer the world offline and off screen. Explore those things! Your devices and online community will be there when you're ready to return to the cyberhive.

MY NEIGHBORHIVE MISSION DEBRIEFING
mission completion date
....

how do you feel after completing the sting operation?

....

....

....

what did you notice afterwards?
- about your mission target
- yourself/team
- surroundings/neighborhive

....

....

....

what will you want to do again with this mission to make your target feel special/that you made a difference?

....

....

....

what ideas do you have for your next sting ops mission?

....

....

....

HELP MAKE SOMEONE'S DREAM (OR HOLIDAY WISH!) COME TRUE
solo op or team op

99

TARGET: Friend, family member, neighbor hiver

TIME: 00:35+

COST: $-$$$

MISSION OBJECTIVE:
Bring long-lasting, memorable joy to an individual or group by *blesSTING* them with a dream or wish!

GEAR & PROVISIONS:
- Giving attitude
- Investigatory skills to find out what his or her dream or holiday wish is
- Whatever supplies or connections you need to make it come to life!

PREP STEP:
Do a little behind-the-scenes ninja work to find out what will really blow the recipient away!

GO TIME!
1. Identify what you can do to make your mission target's wish come true.
2. Gather the necessary resources, but keep the mission under wraps! Ask for help as needed.
3. Spread the sunshine, and bring that dream to life!

TACTICAL SUCCESS KEY:
Preserve the surprise—it's a key ingredient! Capture the reveal on camera if you can!

MY NEIGHBORHIVE MISSION DEBRIEFING
mission completion date ....

how do you feel after completing the sting operation?

....
....

what did you notice afterwards?
- about your mission target
- yourself/team
- surroundings/neighborhive

what will you want to do again with this mission to make your target feel special/that you made a difference?

....
....

what ideas do you have for your next sting ops mission?

....
....

LEARN MORE ABOUT SUSTAINABLE AGRICULTURE AND HOW YOU CAN HELP YOUR COMMUNITY

solo op or team op

100

TARGET: Your community

TIME: 00:45+

COST: $

🎯 MISSION OBJECTIVE:

Learn more about sustainable agriculture and how you can help your community support better practices.

⚙️ GEAR & PROVISIONS:

- Access to online resources or a local library
- An interest in getting to know your local farmer

☑️ PREP STEP:

Visit the farmers' markets in your community, and have fun with your curiosity as you explore each item and stand.

🕐 GO TIME!

1. Learn as much as you can online, in books, and by asking local farmers.

2. Shop at farmers' markets frequently.

3. Find out where your grocery store's produce is sourced to make educated decisions about what you're feeding yourself and your family.

🔑 TACTICAL SUCCESS KEY:

There's always something new to learn. Ask great questions when you have opportunities to talk to your local farmers. Find out the best ways to support sustainable farming practices. Everybody eats—and every dollar we spend on food is a vote. Who is your food voting for?

MY NEIGHBORHIVE MISSION DEBRIEFING
mission completion date

how do you feel after completing the sting operation?

what did you notice afterwards?
- about your mission target
- yourself/team
- surroundings/neighborhive

what will you want to do again with this mission to make your target feel special/that you made a difference?

what ideas do you have for your next sting ops mission?

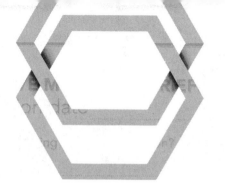

STING-OPS
MISSION TEMPLATES

Use these templates to help you devise and implement your own sting-ops missions. Then share the sunshine by posting your mission idea at blesSTING.com. The sting-ops missions you create will inspire and equip other hivers to keep changing the world for the better!

Additional sting-ops mission templates may be downloaded at blesSTING.com.

MISSION DESCRIPTION:

solo op or team op
(circle one or both, as appropriate)

TARGET:
TIME:
COST:

⌖ MISSION OBJECTIVE:

. . . .
. . . .
. . . .
. . . .

⚙ GEAR & PROVISIONS:

. . . .
. . . .
. . . .
. . . .
. . . .

☑ PREP STEP:

. . . .
. . . .
. . . .
. . . .

⌚ GO TIME!

. . . .
. . . .
. . . .
. . . .

⚷ TACTICAL SUCCESS KEY:

. . . .
. . . .
. . . .

MY NEIGHBORHIVE MISSION DEBRIEFING
mission completion date ....

how do you feel after completing the sting operation?

....

....

....

what did you notice afterwards?

- about your mission target
- yourself/team
- surroundings/neighborhive

....

what will you want to do again with this mission to make your target feel special/that you made a difference?

....

....

....

what ideas do you have for your next sting ops mission?

....

....

....

MISSION DESCRIPTION:

solo op or team op
(circle one or both, as appropriate)

TARGET:
TIME:
COST:

☑ PREP STEP:

. . . .
. . . .
. . . .
. . . .

◎ MISSION OBJECTIVE:

. . . .
. . . .
. . . .

⏱ GO TIME!

. . . .
. . . .
. . . .

⚙ GEAR & PROVISIONS:

. . . .
. . . .
. . . .
. . . .

🔑 TACTICAL SUCCESS KEY:

. . . .
. . . .
. . . .

MY NEIGHBORHIVE MISSION DEBRIEFING
mission completion date

how do you feel after completing the sting operation?

what did you notice afterwards?
- about your mission target
- yourself/team
- surroundings/neighborhive

what will you want to do again with this mission to make your target feel special/that you made a difference?

what ideas do you have for your next sting ops mission?

MISSION DESCRIPTION:

solo op or team op
(circle one or both, as appropriate)

TARGET:
TIME:
COST:

⊙ MISSION OBJECTIVE:

. . . .
. . . .
. . . .
. . . .

⚙ GEAR & PROVISIONS:

. . . .
. . . .
. . . .
. . . .
. . . .

☑ PREP STEP:

. . . .
. . . .
. . . .
. . . .

🕒 GO TIME!

. . . .
. . . .
. . . .
. . . .

🔑 TACTICAL SUCCESS KEY:

. . . .
. . . .
. . . .
. . . .

MY NEIGHBORHIVE MISSION DEBRIEFING
mission completion date ....

how do you feel after completing the sting operation?

....

....

what did you notice afterwards?
- about your mission target
- yourself/team
- surroundings/neighborhive

what will you want to do again with this mission to make your target feel special/that you made a difference?

....

....

what ideas do you have for your next sting ops mission?

....

....

....

MISSION DESCRIPTION:

solo op or team op
(circle one or both, as appropriate)

TARGET:
TIME:
COST:

🎯 MISSION OBJECTIVE:

....
....
....
....

⚙️ GEAR & PROVISIONS:

....
....
....
....
....

☑ PREP STEP:

....
....
....
....

🕒 GO TIME!

....
....
....
....

🔑 TACTICAL SUCCESS KEY:

....
....
....
....

MY NEIGHBORHIVE MISSION DEBRIEFING
mission completion date ....

how do you feel after completing the sting operation?

....

....

....

what did you notice afterwards?
- about your mission target
- yourself/team
- surroundings/neighborhive

....

what will you want to do again with this mission to make your target feel special/that you made a difference?

....

....

....

what ideas do you have for your next sting ops mission?

....

....

....

DARE TO BE A
DIFFERENCE MAKER

Visit blesSTING.com to join the Sting-Ops Underground for updates and access to more great resources to help you *spread the sunshine*. Receive a free digital download of *Dare to be a Difference Maker, Volume 5* as our gift to you!

Instead of dirt and poison, we have rather chosen to fill our hives with honey and wax, thus furnishing mankind with the two noblest of things, which are sweetness and light.

—Jonathan Swift, *The Battle of the Books*

At times, the road to peace can seem anything but peaceful. We find peace not by way of luck or achievement but through authentic connections and what we give of ourselves along the journey. How we experience each footstep is a reflection of each inner thought.

You want love? Give love abundantly. Success? Help others accomplish their dreams. Begin with mindfulness and leading yourself, and every need will be provided. Focus your heart on service and gratitude. In turn, the universe will be yours.

Keep giving, keep growing, and keep going! Because everyone can change the world, right from their own neighborhive!

Thank you for *beeing* you and for all you do!

—Mandy

ABOUT THE AUTHOR

Amanda Ferris is a solution-finding entrepreneur from the Minneapolis area. Thanks to the strong influence of personal-development books and inspirational leaders from an early age, she has always been on the lookout for opportunities to contribute to the world. With her parents' guidance and encouragement, she was challenged to create and present proposals of her ideas as early as age five. She started her career assisting in her mother's day care, where she learned how to build curricula by teaching children in a playful, memorable way. Mandy soon worked her way from what began as a summer job at a neighborhood restaurant to more than ten years of management, service training, and consulting in the hospitality industry.

Mandy is known for her high energy and creativity. Her dedication to lifelong learning and the pay-it-forward philosophy truly shines in her training and development programs. She volunteers with local organizations to help high school students prepare for their future careers and cultivate their entrepreneurial skills. Mandy also enjoys being a coach, pinup artist, and voiceover talent. In her free time, she travels the world, bakes, and loves time spent outdoors.

All proceeds from sales of this book will benefit organizations that support veterans of the US armed forces and local law enforcement officers to help the families of those who have served or currently serve. They have sacrificed so much so that we may enjoy freedom and safer communities as we work together to make the world a better place.

Thank you for supporting our heroes.

RISE AND SHINE!

Go. Do. *Bee!*